THE EAGLE IS FORGOTTEN

FORGOTTEN

Pierre Eugène Du Simitière, Founding Father of American Numismatics

BY DR. JOEL J. OROSZ

Foreword By Eric P. Newman

THE EAGLE THAT IS FORGOTTEN

Pierre Eugène Du Simitière, Founding Father of American Numismatics

BY DR. JOEL J. OROSZ

Foreword By Eric P. Newman

Published By:

BOWERS AND MERENA GALLERIES, INC.
Box 1224, Wolfeboro, New Hampshire 03894

ISBN 0-943161-08-8 (paperback)
ISBN 0-943161-16-9 (hardbound)

The Eagle That Is Forgotten
By Dr. Joel J. Orosz

Published By:
Bowers and Merena Galleries, Inc.
Box 1224
Wolfeboro, New Hampshire 03894

Cover: George Washington, engraving after an original drawing by Du Simitiere.

TABLE OF CONTENTS

ACKNOWLEDGMENTS

The author wishes to thank Gordon M. Marshall, the assistant librarian of the Library Company of Philadelphia, who assisted my research in ways too numerous to mention. Michael Hodder and Tom Becker of Bowers and Merena Galleries generously provided research help on certain topics. Eric P. Newman, the dean of scholars in the field of early American numismatics, provided—in addition to his superb foreword—a painstaking critical reading of the manuscript, which eliminated many errors; Mr. Newman also offered many valuable insights that have been incorporated into this work. Q. David Bowers should be thanked in a thousand ways: as a patient patron; an enthusiastic publisher; a careful research partner; and an insightful critical reader. Together, Messrs. Newman and Bowers corrected many errors; those that remain are the sole responsibility of the author.

FOREWORD

The courage of a true collector of knowledge and "things" is reflected in the absorbing experiences of Pierre Eugène Du Simitière in America. As a late 18th-century resident of various American communities he was a true dilettante with an insatiable appetite for accumulating and studying all types of tangible collectibles available to a person with no economic advantages. His talent and work as a designer and artist did not seem to divert his cultural devotion to being an enthusiastic "pack rat" with a mission.

Joel J. Orosz, as evidenced by his research and writings about Du Simitière, is obviously a great admirer of that remarkable individual for his myriad of interests, for his desire to seek constant cultural excitement and for his devotion to sharing his achievements with the public—and also undertaking these projects singlehandedly. Orosz does not use success as a standard of admiration but recognizes the magnitude of tireless effort to overcome frustration and impossible odds as a measure of Du Simitière's importance. This book is a presentation of the numismatic achievements of Du Simitière. It is an opportunity for a sophisticated reader to take a refreshing look backward to the beginnings of numismatics in America. One can appreciate how Orosz has made Du Simitière the numismatist live again if one puts oneself in the time and place setting of that unusual foreigner in America.

— Eric P. Newman

St. Louis, Missouri
March 24, 1988

AUTHOR'S NOTE

The author first learned of Pierre Eugène Du Simitière in 1982, while conducting research for his doctoral dissertation on the early history of American museums. Contributions made by the Swiss virtuoso to the development of American museums have been acknowledged by the author and by other historians of museums, but Du Simitière's role as a founding father of numismatics in this country has been virtually forgotten.

The following pages tell the story of Du Simitière, as much as is possible, in his own words. Quotations are transcribed *exactly* as Du Simitière wrote them, with the erratic spelling, punctuation, and capitalization of 18th-century American English preserved without comment, excepting occasional explanations for the sake of clarity.

His life was replete with ironies. One of the greatest is that Du Simitière, a portraitist by profession, and a man who owned several pictures of eminent men, apparently never did a self-portrait. Nor, it seems, did any other artist take the virtuoso's likeness, for no reliable image of him is known to survive. Another notable irony is that the site of Du Simitière's last home in Philadelphia—at Arch above Fourth Street—is literally a stone's throw away from the present-day Philadelphia Mint.

The saddest irony is that Du Simitière, a man who died a pauper and who was buried in an unmarked Philadelphia grave, fathered an avocation whose very name today is synonymous with wealth. This little book does not pretend to fully explain the odd enigma that was Pierre Eugène Du Simitière. It does, however, shed some light on his numismatic achievements, which comprise a legacy that deserves to be remembered by every numismatist.

DEDICATION

For Florence, who has been so supportive.

"The Eagle That Is Forgotten":

Pierre Eugène Du Simitière, Founding Father of American Numismatics

Sleep softly...eagle forgotten...
  under the stone,
Time has its way with you there, and
  the clay has its own.
Sleep on, O brave-hearted, O wise man,
  that kindled the flame—
To live in mankind is far more than to
  live in a name.

"The Eagle That Is Forgotten"—Vachel Lindsay

*   *   *   *   *   *   *

"...at this time, [ca. 1772] I became acquainted with Mr. Simitere a miniature painter, he was fond of collecting objects of natural History, his painting room was ornamented with frames of Butterflies, and he had a considerable number of Snakes & C. in spirits—he also collected medals and coins. he was a Batchler and such was his chief amusement."[1]

There is more than a little professional jealousy evident in this letter written, in 1812, by Charles Willson Peale to his son, Rembrandt. Like Peale, Pierre Eugène Du Simitière (1737-1784) was an artist and the proprietor of a pioneering museum in Philadelphia. Peale had more talent in the first line and more success in the latter, but it always rankled him that Du Simitière had preceded him in both endeavors. Peale nevertheless admitted that Du Simitière's coins formed "a valuable collection."[2] Even this, however, is an understatement. Pierre Eugène Du Simitière was among the first in America to form a substantial collection of coinage, both American and foreign, as well as paper money. While building his collection, this Swiss emigré had dealings with other collectors in Burlington (New Jersey), New York City, and Philadelphia, thus revealing that the first seeds of numismatics were planted in America well before the Revolution. Du Simitière's knowledge of heraldry and his artistic ability made him a natural choice to be the first consultant on medals to the fledgling United States, and his suggestions have greatly influenced both the devices and the mottos of our coins and paper money down to the present period. His portrait of Washington, taken from life, was used and reused on Washington pieces. He aspired to be one of the first numismatic authors in America, and if one counts unpublished manuscripts, he succeeded. Finally, he was directly, if unwillingly, responsible for this nation's earliest known auction of coins and paper money. Pierre Eugène Du Simitière, an associate of John Adams, Benjamin Franklin, and Thomas Jefferson, truly was a founding father of numismatics in America, but he is almost utterly obscure today. This undeserved oblivion is totally unjustifiable, for, as we shall see, the "eagle that is forgotten" exerted tremendous influence over the future course of American numismatics.

Birth of a Collector

Pierre Eugène Du Simitière was born in Geneva, Switzerland, on September 18, 1737, the son of Jean-Henri Ducimetière and Judith-Ulrique-Cunegonde Delormé. Jean-Henri was a broker in the East Indies trade, and it was perhaps this exposure to foreign nations that led his son, in 1757, to leave Europe for the new world. Young Pierre's intention was to write a guide to the natural history of the Caribbean Islands, illustrated by his own drawings. From 1757 to 1763 he embarked on an odyssey of research, visiting every major island in that region, collecting specimens for his proposed natural history. Soon he expanded the scope of his efforts to a civil and natural history of the Caribbean and England's North American provinces. In the 11 years from 1763 to 1774, Du Simitière moved 12 times, on every occasion taking his drawing collection with him.[3] By 1774, when he settled permanently in Philadelphia, Du Simitière had formed a small but respectable private cabinet of natural history specimens, works of art, coins, medals, and books.

A piece of evidence in the Du Simitière papers at the Library Company of Philadelphia suggests that the young Swiss began collecting the coins very early in his travels. He prepared a nine-page manuscript titled *"Des Manières de Compteu & des Monnoyer des Isles du Vent & Sous le Vent."*[4] Like the title, the text is written in French, and it comprises one of the first attempts to produce numismatic literature in America. In fact, since Du Simitière wrote it sometime between the years 1763 and 1774, this work is older than the United States itself. Du Simitière tried to identify the type of monetary system used by each nation (for instance, Jamaica used the British system while Puerto Rico used that of Spain) and then delineated the relative values of money in each island in the West Indies. He compiled a chart showing the comparative values of English, French, Dutch, Spanish, and Portuguese coins in Caribbean commerce, and annotated it with the slang names of coins in the different islands. A Spanish piastre (peso), according to his charts, was worth 10 French sols (one sol equalled one-twentieth livre). A sol, according to his notes, was referred to as a "dritje" on Dutch islands.[5] Du Simitière recorded much valuable information about West Indies coinage in his manuscript, but he was never able to discipline himself sufficiently to actually publish his findings. This, regrettably, was a pattern he followed all of his life. Still, his contribution deserves recognition for its pioneering nature.

Du Simitière's Patron, John Smith

Part of Du Simitière's problem was his inability to stay in one place. Just as he moved every few months from island to island in the West Indies, so he moved from city to city with the same frequency during his sojourn in America, beginning in New York during the year 1763. Du Simitière's itinerant lifestyle, however, was not devoid of purpose; it was in fact part wanderlust and part calculation. Every city had something different to offer his collection, and he collected freely in every city. He also kept an eye open for a patron wherever he wandered, for his tastes constantly outran his pocketbook. Not long after his arrival in America, possibly as early as 1763, Du Simitière found such a man, one John Smith of Burlington, New Jersey.[6] Smith was a Quaker merchant of some means. He was also, by happy chance, an early numismatist. Du Simitière remembered after Smith's death that his friend's coin collection "was considerable."[7] The two apparently hit it off well, for Smith became Du Simitière's patron; in the words of the Swiss, Smith was his "friend and protector."[8]

The two men carried on a happy numismatic relationship. In fact, their surviving correspondence covers no subject other than coins. On November 21, 1766, Du Simitière turned the tables on his patron and made Smith a numismatic gift:

> You will find also a few copper coins [in a package that Du Simitière was sending to Smith] though none of the most curious, yet Such as I have them to Spare. I thought they might find a corner in your drawers as they require but little room, you will find the explanation of them in their respective papers.[9]

Unfortunately, neither the coins nor the papers have survived. We can, however, make an informed guess as to the identity of some of these pieces. Since Du Simitière sent Smith coins "Such as I have them to Spare," we can assume that they were duplicates. As it happened, Du Simitière made a list of coins that were in his collection in Philadelphia on March 17, 1767, fewer than four months after he wrote the above-quoted letter. His list totaled "380 monnoyes & medailles diverses en ma possession le 17 Mars 1767 à Philadelphia," of which there were "180 pieces de'argent" [silver], "176 de cuivre," [copper] and "24 d'or" [gold]. The list gives only very general descriptions of his coins, but some solid information can be gleaned from it. Among his silver holdings were 47 English, 18 German, 14 Danish, 16 French, and 13 Spanish coins. His copper strikings included 16 French, 25 German and Dutch, 12 Portuguese and Spanish, and even 11 Russian, Swedish, Polish, and Chinese coins. There were eight "inconnes" [unknowns], an indication of the paucity of numismatic information available to Du Simitière. We can safely assume that the Swiss sent John Smith duplicates of pieces such as these.[10]

The next correspondence between Du Simitière and his patron regarded the collection of another numismatist, a "Major James" of Philadelphia. Efforts to discover more about Major James have proved fruitless, but he apparently had a notable collection by the standards of the time, for Smith asked Du Simitière to make an evaluation of it. Du Simitière carried out his patron's request in a letter of August 6, 1767:

> According to my promise when I had the honor to be with you lately, I will now give you an account of the collection of Coins in Major James's possession, which has not been in my power to do before, as he was for some weeks out of town after my arrival heere, but Since his return, having been frequently entertained in his house, I have had the opportunity of viewing his medals several times, the greatest part of them consists of Charthaginians or Punicks, greeks & Imperial Roman, which the major collected chiefly at Gibraltar from the ruins of [an] ancient city in the neighbourhood named *Cartera* which was founded by the carthaginians and afterwards made a colony by the Romans, the History and antiquities of that place have been the Study of that gentleman for Some years and he is about putting it in order for the press. he has also some curious moresco or arabic coins in Silver and copper found in the Same place of which you have inclosed a small specimen. of modern medals he has but few, & Such only as are got here & there by chance & no Set of them, there is Some ancient Saxon and english coin much older than any I have but they are not compleat. as for what he purchased lately there were only modern German coins of various sorts amongst which were many lyon-dollars which are no curiosity. I have made no addition to my Stock that way but Such as the generosity of the major has bestowed on me, chiefly ancient.[11]

Du Simitière's letter reveals several tantalizing tidbits. Major James was obviously a donor to Du Simitière's collection, and an antiquarian of some diligence, but not a systematic collector, for he collected "by chance." Major James seems to have gathered the bulk of his collection in the Old World, for his recent purchases had been limited to "modern German coins," which were not unusual in the American provinces. Most interesting of all, however, the letter establishes that in 1767, there were at least three serious numismatists in the Philadelphia area.

Coins brought Du Simitière and John Smith together in other ways, as evidenced by a letter the Swiss wrote to Smith's son-in-law, William Dillwyn, shortly after his patron had died. "I See that your late father in law acquainted you with a parcel of Silver medals and coins I deposited with him at my return from N. York," Du Simitière began. He went on to explain that these coins were:

> A consideration for a Sum he was so generous as to lend me the year before, these coins which I delivered him in a paper Sealed and directed to himself were in number [one] hundred and thirty five, collected during many years at no small expense, many of whom being Scarce cost'd me much more than their weight. I gave him at the Same time a catalog of them which you'll no doubt will find among his papers.[12]

The dates of the loan and the delivery of the numismatic material can be established with some certainty. Du Simitière says that he gave Smith the coins on his "return from N. York," and that he had borrowed the money the year before that. The Swiss moved from New York to Burlington, New Jersey in 1770, so the coins were undoubtedly transferred then. That would fix the date of the loan as 1769. This all fits with the date of the letter to Dillwyn, which was written in 1771. It comes as no surprise that Du Simitière found it necessary to take a loan, for he was always short of cash, due largely to his extravagance in buying items for his collection. It is interesting to note that even in the 1760s, it was necessary to pay a premium to secure scarce coins. Most importantly, however, the catalogue Du Simitière sent to Smith has survived. It indeed lists 135 coins and medals, which, while not a priceless collection by any means, did come from a surprisingly large variety of eras and countries.[13]

This friendly and mutually beneficial association came to an end on March 26, 1771, when Smith died at the age of 49. His loss was a blow to Du Simitière, who poured out his grief in a letter to a friend:

> I thought I should acquaint you with the great loss I have Sustain'd by the death of my much respected friend Mr. John Smith of Burlington, after several months of a lingering illness, as you have heard me frequently Speak of him, you may easily form yourSelf an Idea of my sorrows in losing So good a friend and protector...[14]

It seems safe to assume that one of the reasons for Du Simitière's sadness was the fact that his coins were now at the mercy of Smith's executor, his son-in-law, William Dillwyn. Only eight days after Smith's death, Dillwyn wrote Du Simitière. This letter is lost, but the tone of Du Simitière's reply would suggest that Dillwyn demanded repayment of the loan, a demand with which the impecunious Swiss could not comply. Du Simitière's reply, dated April 7, 1771, is almost plaintive in tone:

> I am very confident that if providence had continued him [Smith] among us I should have had them [the coins] again for the Same Sum whenever it would have been convenient for me to have repaid it, but as it has pleased the almighty to dispose of him before [I] could terminate that affair, I must now Submit to part with them for ever as it is not at present in my power to repay that sum to his executors. I acknowledge here with gratitude your kindness for me in following So far the intentions of that very respectable gentleman in offering them to me upon the terms I had agreed with him and I find my Self unfortunate in not being able to accept of your generous offer. I imagine however that they'll remain with you or Some of the family at least for Some time as well as his own collection which was considerable and would flatter my self that if they Should ever come to be Sold, you or the next of his executors would (in consideration of the friendship with which that worthy gentleman had honoured me for Several years past) favour me with the first offer.[15]

Du Simitière was to be disappointed in his wish. William Dillwyn later wrote the following words on the back of the catalogue of Du Simitière's 135 coins:

> 10 mo. 23d. 1772. The bundle of Coins and Medals herein mentioned and a Copy of the List, Wm. Dillwyn took to Phila. with him in Order to put them into the hands of Jos. Richardson, Goldsmith there, to sell, and acct. for them to the Executor.[16]

Dillwyn had waited more than a year and a half, presumably for Du Simitière to find the money to reclaim the coins, but in vain. Joseph Richardson, Sr., was a Quaker silversmith whose son, Joseph Richardson, Jr., took over the family business upon his retirement in 1777. The younger Richardson achieved numismatic immortality by engraving several versions of the beautiful "George Washington President" 1793 Indian Peace Medal.[17] Now, however, we must include the elder Richardson in the annals of numismatic history, for another notation by Dillwyn on the back of the catalogue simply reads "List of Medals and Coins (sold Wm. Logan)."[18] Thus Joseph Richardson, Sr. around late 1772 or early 1773, conducted the earliest known sale, in America, of a collection of coins by private treaty.[19] To place this into historical perspective, Americans were still subjects of the British crown, and the first coin

The Eagle That Is Forgotten

auction discovered by Attinelli was still at least 55 years in the future.[20]

The "William Logan" who bought the coins was the grandson of James Logan, (1674-1751) a jurist and politician who was an advisor to William Penn and, from 1736 to 1738, the acting governor of the province of Pennsylvania. He was also John Smith's nephew, for the Quaker merchant had married Hannah Logan, James Logan's daughter, in 1748. Efforts to trace Du Simitière's coins through descendants of the Logan family proved unavailing, however, and the trail of the Du Simitière/Smith coins ends with William Logan.[21]

The relationship between Smith and Du Simitière reveals many important facts about American numismatic history. First, there were coin collectors in the 1760s in at least two cities; Philadelphia and Burlington, New Jersey, and they were aware of each other's existence. (In addition to Major James, Smith, and Du Simitière in the Philadelphia area, there was in Boston a fourth numismatist, Rev. Andrew Eliot; it is not known if Eliot was aware of the Philadelphians, or vice-versa).[22] Second, rare coins were trading at a premium in America 10 years before the Revolution. Third, Joseph Richardson, Sr. held the first known sale of a coin collection by private treaty in America more than five decades before the coin trade as such is presumed to have "begun to begin" in America.

Du Simitière's Coin Lists

The loss of 135 silver coins to the Smith estate certainly reduced Du Simitière's numismatic holdings, but by no means did it exhaust them. Du Simitière was an inveterate list maker. In addition to the list of his numismatic collection mentioned above, dated March 17, 1767, and his catalogue of the 135 coins forfeited to the Smith estate, the Swiss left behind four dated and five undated lists detailing his coin collection. All of the dated lists were made before the loss of the coins to Smith's estate, and they reveal a sizeable collection; for instance, in New York, on February 7, 1769, he possessed 522 pieces "en tout", of which 252 were copper, 240 silver, and 30 gold.[23] Thus the loss of 135 coins still left him with a considerable collection. (Four of the undated lists are reproduced as appendices 1-4.)

The undated lists go into somewhat more detail. There is a separate list apiece for British coins, ancient coins, Roman medals, and "ancient & modern gold medals & coins," all of which delineate a wide variety of material, most of which is relatively common today.[24] None of the lists can be dated with certainty because the latest-dated coin on any of them was struck in 1765. The fifth list provides a delightful glimpse of the wide range of Du Simitière's collecting interests. Entitled "List of Curiosities to be Found in Philadelphia," it is mainly a record of additions to Du Simitière's private cabinet. Mixed in with such numismatic entries as "un Farthing de George I, 1720" are such colorful notations as "a piece of Sugar made out of the mapple tree in Nova Scotia.[25] Nineteen coins are enumerated in this list. While none of these records reveal any earthshaking rarities, one must admire Du Simitière's diligence in tracking down these coins in America, so far from their points of origin, and in collecting them at a time of dearth of hard coin in circulation. It is especially remarkable, in light of the chronic specie shortage, that his list of gold coins and medals contains 24 entries. (See fig. 1a.)

Du Simitière and Numismatic Literature

Du Simitière was a voracious collector, perhaps even a hoarder, but he was no mere pack rat. He constantly sought information about his acquisitions, and built up a small, but effective numismatic library. Among his books were Pierre Bizot's *Medallische Historie der Republyk van Holland* (Amsterdam: 1690),[26] and an entry in his "List of Curiosities to be Found in Philadelphia" suggests that he owned a book entitled *"The Metallick History of King William & Q. Mary Queen Ann [sic] & King George I fo. fig."*[27] We do know that he made extracts of two of the leading numismatic texts of the time, James Simon's *Essay Towards an Historical Account of Irish Coins* (Dublin: 1749) and Stephen Martin Leake's *Historical Account of English Money* (London: 2nd edition, 1745), which suggests that he did not own the actual books, but had read them.

Du Simitière's extract of Simon is brief and straightforward, consisting mainly of helpful facts, such as, "the harp does not appear on Irish coins before Henry VIII."[28] This précis is also carefully cross-referenced to the *Philosophical Transactions* and to Leake's *Historical Account of English Money.*

Du Simitière's extracts of Leake's book are far more extensive and of great historical importance. There are two extracts of Leake in Du Simitière's handwriting. The first, in the Library of Congress, is a factual gleaning from Leake's book, and concentrates wholly on English coinage.[29] The second, in the Library Company of Philadelphia, is much more significant, for it is annotated by Du Simitière with information and stories of his own experiences.[30] This extract deserves a detailed examination.

The first section of Leake's work that Du Simitière extracted was "New England Money." Du Simitière noted of the "New England" (NE) coinage that "those were the first money coin'd in New England from the plate brought in by the trade and the plunder of the buccaneers or pirates."[31] This interesting observation is not specifically supported, but may be at least partially true. Du Simitière went on to record several historically important facts about the New England coinage. "I have Seen several two pences," the Swiss began, "and I have observ'd upon all the dates to be 1662, which is the more remarkable,

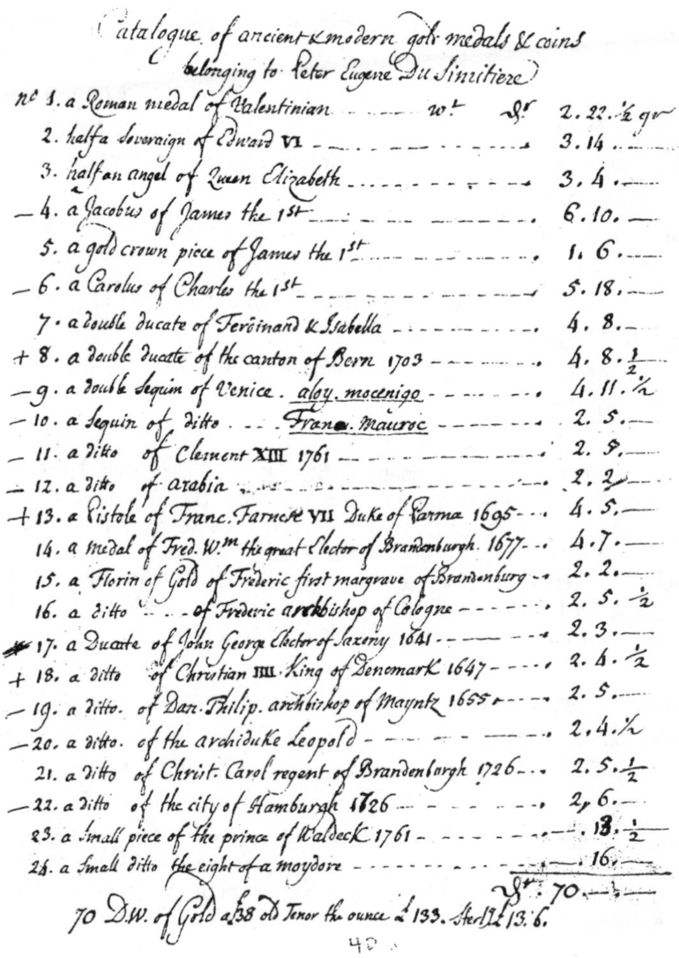

Catalogue of ancient & modern gold medals & coins
belonging to Peter Eugene Du Simitière)

n° 1. a Roman medal of Valentinian .... w.t ℥. 2. 22. ½ gr
2. half a sovereign of Edward VI - - - - - - - - - - - - 3. 14. ...
3. half an angel of Queen Elizabeth - - - - - - - - 3. 4. ——
— 4. a Jacobus of James the 1st - - - - - - - - - - 6. 10. ——
5. a gold crown piece of James the 1st - - - - - - 1. 6. ——
— 6. a Carolus of Charles the 1st - - - - - - - - - 5. 18. ——
7. a double ducate of Ferdinand & Isabella - - - - - - - 4. 8. —
+ 8. a double ducate of the canton of Bern 1703 - - - - - - 4. 8. ½
— 9. a double sequin of Venice. aloy. mocenigo - - - - - - 4. 11. ½
— 10. a sequin of ditto - - - Franc. mauroc - - - - - - 2. 5. —
— 11. a ditto of Clement XIII 1761 - - - - - - - 2. 9.
— 12. a ditto of arabia ... - - - - - - - - - 2. 2.
+ 13. a pistole of Franc. Farnese VII Duke of Parma 1695 - - - 4. 5. ——
14. a medal of Fred. W.m the great Elector of Brandenburgh. 1677 - - 4. 7. ——
15. a florin of gold of Frederic first margrave of Brandenburg - - 2. 2. ——
16. a ditto - - - - of Frederic archbishop of Cologne - - - - - - 2. 5. ½
17. a ducate of John George Elector of Saxony 1641 - - - - - 2. 3. ——
+ 18. a ditto of Christian IIII King of Denemark 1647 - - - - 2. 4. ½
— 19. a ditto of Dan. Philip. archbishop of Mayntz 1655 - - - - 2. 5. ——
— 20. a ditto of the archiduke Leopold - - - - - - - - - 2. 4. ½
21. a ditto of Christ. Carol regent of Brandenborgh 1726 - - - 2. 5. ½
— 22. a ditto of the city of Hamburgh 1726 - - - - - - 2, 6. ——
23. a small piece of the prince of Waldeck 1761 - - - - - - 13. ½
24. a small ditto the eight of a moydore - - - - - - - - - 16.
℥.t 70.
70 D.W. of Gold at 38 old Tenor the ounce £ 133. Sterl. £ 13. 6.
40.

Figure 1A

Catalogue of Ancient and Modern Gold Medals and Coins Belonging to Peter Eugène Du Simitière.

One of Du Simitière's undated lists. He occasionally anglicized his first name, rendering "Pierre" as "Peter." (Courtesy, Library Company of Philadelphia.)

as it has been entirely unnoticed by all writers..."[32] Du Simitière was not quite correct on this point—an engraving of the 1662 Oak Tree twopence from the Pembroke Collection had been prepared in the 1720s, and was sold in 1746—but his source was at fault. Leake, on page 349 of his second edition, stated that *all* twopences bore the date 1652. So Du Simitière did not discover the Oak Tree twopence, but he did, at least, correct Leake on the matter of its date. The Swiss also sketched the coin for his collection, as shown in fig. 1. Interestingly, the fact that Du Simitière considered it remarkable that (as he believed) no other writer had discovered the Oak Tree twopence, suggests that coins were a matter of some interest to the intellectuals of provincial American society.

Turning to the New England shillings, Du Simitière corrected another of Leake's errors, a claim that there existed octangular shillings. Du Simitière debunked that myth, saying, "I have never Seen any of the Octangular Sort, not even in the [prints?] of them"[33].

The Swiss went on to note the tribulations suffered by the Massachusetts shilling in commerce:

> The value of these pieces is ninepence Sterling or a Shilling lawfull money of New England were they are current to this day (1775) altho many of them [are] very much Clipt. but I have Seen Some So good as to weigh near tenpence Sterling...The original weight and value Should have been10d. Sterling but [they] are now reduced to 9d. on account of the clipping. for I was told in Boston that a man there had a Silver Tankard made, only of the clippings of the New England Shillings.[34]

Obviously, clipping was big business in colonial times, for a tankard required a considerable amount of silver to fabricate. Du Simitière continued his section on New England money by making this intriguing statement:

> there is pennys with a tree but [I] am not certain whether there is any of the plain ones. they are extremely Scarce—as well as shillings of the first sort plain with XII & NE for in a bag of about three Thousand in the treasurer's office in Boston, I could find but one.[35]

By "plain ones" Du Simitière meant the "New England" coins, the fields of which were mostly empty (see fig.1). He was mistaken, however, as to the existence of "Pine Tree" or "Oak Tree" pennies, but once again, Du Simitière's error was copied directly from a standard reference, Sir Martin Folkes' *Tables of English and Gold Coins* (London: 1745).[36] DuSimitière was equally taken in by the "Good Samaritan Shilling," also illustrated by Folkes, for he accepted its existence even as he noted that "the piece as far as I was

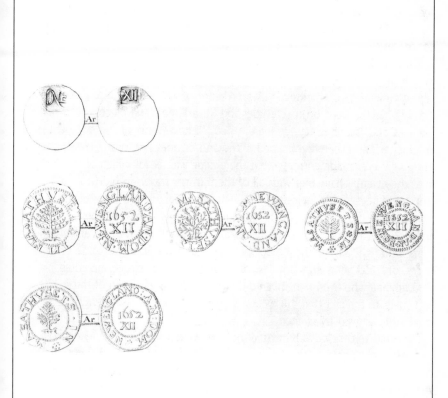

Figure 1

Du Simitière's Sketches of New England and Massachusetts Coinage.

Top row: Obverse and reverse of 1652 New England shilling.

Second row: Obverses and reverses of three coins: a Massachusetts Pine Tree shilling, Noe-3 (a very rare variety, an example of which was Lot 1216 in *Garrett III*; an Oak Tree shilling, Noe-1, (an example of which was sold as Lot 1204 in *Garrett III*); a Massachusetts Small Planchet Pine Tree shilling.

Third row: Obverse and reverse of a Massachusetts Large Planchet Pine Tree shilling.

These superb drawings prove Du Simitière could distinguish among minute differences in the varieties of coinage. (Courtesy, Library Company of Philadelphia.)

The Eagle That Is Forgotten

able to learn is now unknown in New England."[37] By far the most interesting part of the former statement, however, concerns Du Simitière's method
of collecting coins. He found that the NE shillings were rare by searching through
bags of coins in the treasurer's office, in quest of additional pieces for his collection. This passage, written in 1775, places Du Simitière second only to Rev.
Andrew Eliot in launching a systematic effort to collect coins in America (see
footnote 22).

Du Simitière continued his extract of Leake with "Maryland Money," in
which he mentioned the Lord Baltimore coinage and "Plantation Money,"
about which he commented, "I never heard of any Such before I read this
book."[38] Leake went on to consider the Rosa Americana pieces, both halfpennies and farthings. Du Simitière noted, "I have some of the half pennys
in Copper," and then complained, "The author does not inform us whether
they were ever made current, what their value was, & for which of the colonies they were. I have met with all of them in my travels in North America,
but could never learn their use."[39] Du Simitière indeed met with Rosa Americana pieces in his travels, for he carefully illustrated different types, as seen
in fig. 2. It is interesting to note the negligible impact upon Americans of William Wood's Rosa Americana coinage; although Du Simitière came on the
scene only 30 years after the last of these pieces was struck, he could not
find anyone who even *remembered* them in circulation. Much of this is due,
of course, to the fact that these coins were never shipped to America in bulk,
but rather arrived by chance.

Du Simitière concluded his extract of Leake with a mention of Virginia coinage. After an accurate description of the halfpenny (he made no mention of
the heavier "Penny" or the silver shilling because these are patterns with which
Americans of the Revolutionary era had no contact), he stated:

> I have inquired after this coin for my collection and have been informed
> by a gentleman who had it from one of the virginia delegates to the con-
> tinental congress in July last [1775] that this copper coin had never been
> admitted as a currency in the Colony of Virginia.[40]

This passage is accurate, for most of the Virginia halfpennies did not get
into circulation until after the Revolutionary War.[41] It is, however, interesting
to note that Du Simitière's collecting was so active. It is no wonder that his
quest for both numismatic information and for the coins themselves resulted
in his gathering a respectable collection.

Du Simitière, Numismatic Author

Du Simitière did more than read numismatic literature, he aspired to write

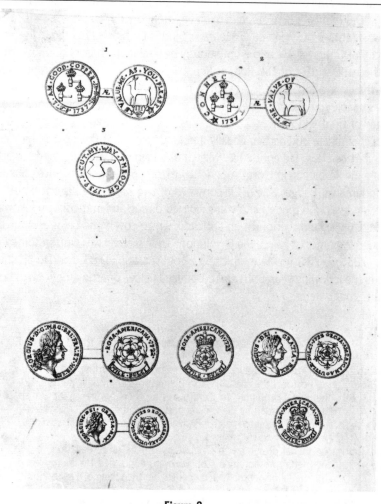

Figure 2

Du Simitière's Drawings of Higley Coppers and Rosa Americana Coinage.

Top row: Higley 1737 threepence, "VALUE ME AS YOU PLEASE"—3 Hammers—"I AM GOOD COPPER"; Higley 1737 threepence, "THE VALUE OF THREE PENCE"—3 Hammers—"CONNECTICVT."

Second row: Higley 1739 threepence, "VALUE ME AS YOU PLEASE"—Broad Axe—"J CUT MY WAY THROUGH." Du Simitière owned, at one time, seven of these extreme rarities, one of the greatest accumulations ever owned by a single numismatist. By contrast, both the Sylvester Sage Crosby Collection and the Garrett Collection contained "only" five specimens. Presumably, these three varieties were among the seven in Du Simitière's cabinet.

Third row: Rosa Americana coins, including the 1722 twopence with no period after "Rex"; the 1723 twopence (reverse only); the 1722 penny with "Utile Dulci" legend.

Fourth row: the 1722 twopence, with period after "Rex"; and the 1723 penny (reverse only). These underweight coins were never accepted by the American people. (Courtesy, Library Company of Philadelphia.)

The Eagle That Is Forgotten

it, and became one of America's earliest numismatic authors. That claim rests on *"Des Manieres de Compteu..."* earlier mentioned, and also on a one-page essay entitled *"Origine de la Monnoye"* in his *Common Place Book* in the Library of Congress. He began ambitiously by tracing the history of money from "the earliest days of the Roman Republic," but the narrative abruptly ends at the close of one page.[42] As with so many of his other projects, Du Simitière was unable to finish this one; it was probably terminated by his chronic shortages of time and money.

Du Simitière outlined an equally ambitious project at the close of his *Common Place Book*. He entitled it "Sketch of a Plan of a Work intended to illustrate the Revolution in North America by Medals, Seals, Coins, Devices, Statues, Monuments, Badges & C..." It consisted of two parts; the historical outline, which deals with medals and coins emitted during and immediately following the struggle, and, curiously, an appendix which covers the coins and medals issued for America *before* the Revolution. The "sketch" was written sometime in 1783 or 1784, for he mentioned a coin struck in 1783, and Du Simitière died the following year. Both are reproduced below, omitting mention of nonnumismatic items:

Historical Outline

1st. the Device and mottos on the Various emissions of the Continental paper money.

2d. the *medal* intended for Gen. Washington on the British army evacuating Boston. [the "Washington Before Boston" medal, Betts 542]

6th. the medal presented to Gen. Gates on the Capture of the British army commanded by Gen. Burgoyne, at Saratoga, 1777. [Betts 557]

7th. the medal presented to Gen. Wayne on the Storming of Stony Point, 1779. [Betts 565]

8th. the medal presented to Col. Fleury on the same occasion.

9th. the medal presented to Col. St. evard (who died the Same year).

10th. the medal presented to Colonel Lee on the taking of Paulus-Hook. [Betts 575]

12th. the medals given to Gen. Morgan and Lieut. Col. Howard on the capture of Col. Tarleton. [Possibly Betts 596]

14th. the *medal* Sent from the Government of England to be distributed among the Indians to encourage them to go to war against the americans.

15th. the *medal* Struck by order of the State of Virginia to be given to the friendly Indians in opposition to the above-mentioned.

16th. the medal Struck at Paris by order of Dr. Franklin, to commemorate the Independence of the United States of America. [The "Libertas Americana" medal, Betts 615]

17th. the *medal* Struck in Holland to commemorate the treaty of Peace between the belligerent Powers.

17a. the medal Struck at Leuwarden in Friesland, on the occasion of that Province having been the first to declare in favor of the American Independence. [Betts 602]

The Eagle That Is Forgotten

17b. the medal Struck at Amsterdam, on the treaty between the United Provinces of the Netherlands and the United States of america. [Probably Betts 604 or 605]

18th. a Coin of the size of a Crown with devices and mottos taken from the continental paper money, Struckt in London on Type-Metal, and dated 1776. [A Continental dollar, although it was not struck in London]

19th. Shillings and Six Pences, of Silver, Struck at annapolis by J. Chalmers, 1783.

20th. Coins privately Struck in Philadelphia with continental devices on them. [Probably the 1783 Nova Constellatio patterns in silver. Although three varieties of Nova Constellatio coppers are dated 1783, they were probably struck in 1785 by George Wyon in Birmingham, England (see footnote 78)].

Appendix

—the Silver plate given by Charles II to the Indian Queen of Pamunkee Virga. [This piece is discussed in detail later]

15th. the brass coins Struck by Mr. Wood for the American colonies, 1722. 1723. [Wood's Hibernia coinage]

16th. the Copper Coins with a Deer, Supposed to have been Struck in Connecticut 1737. [Higley coppers]

17th. the Copper Coin struck at the Tower of London for Virginia 1774 [The Virginia halfpenny, dated 1773, but not actually delivered to the treasurer of Virginia until 1774]

18th. the Medals occasionally given by the Crown of England to the Indians. One Struck by a Society of People, Chiefly Quakers, in Philadelphia to be given to the Indians during the late French War. [Probably the medal produced by the "Friendly Association for Preserving Peace with the Indians by Pacific Measures," a medal struck by Joseph Richardson, Sr., (Betts 401), discussed in footnote 19]

19th. the Medal of William Penn, founder of Pennsylvania, Struck in England by his descendents.

20th. Spanish Silver coins of Phillip II found in a field near Reading [.] NB the New England coins Struck at Boston [in] 1652 as likewise Lord Baltimore's coin from Maryland will only be noticed in their respective places, as they are already delineated in Martin Folkes's *Tables of English Silver and Gold Coins* pag. 91.[43]

After taking into consideration the lack of published references and the non-existence of networks of other collectors, Du Simitière's list is surprisingly complete. The endorsement for the entire plan, which Du Simitière wrote on the overside of his list, tells at once of his ambitions and their failure: "Plans of a Work of illustrating the Revolution of America by Devices, Medals, Coins & C. that have been published on the occasion of the Revolution both in America and in Europe by P.E. Du Simitière."[44] This ambitious plan, which would have been a significant contribution to the knowledge of early American coinage nearly a century before Crosby, was left in this outline form at Du Simitière's death.

The American Museum

It is perhaps inevitable that a man like Du Simitière, who collected art works, books, coins, natural history specimens, historical artifacts and a host of curiosities, would eventually find himself awash in his own collection, and unable to adequately support himself. As the Revolution was coming to an end, in the late autumn of 1781, Du Simitière's collection threatened to crowd him out of his home, and his creditors threatened to evict him. A solution to both problems seemed obvious. He would turn his treasures into a museum, charge for entry, and make the collection pay for itself. Accordingly, in April of 1782, Du Simitière established the "American Museum" at his home on Arch above Fourth Street in Philadelphia.[45] The broadside announcing the opening of the museum is reproduced as fig. 3.

In point of fact, visitors had been coming to view Du Simitière's collection for years; the first recorded guest was Richard Smith, a member of the Continental Congress, who called on September 28, 1775.[46] Now, however, Du Simitière was labeling his collection a "museum" and, more importantly, charging for the privilege of seeing it. For 50 cents, a visitor received a tour from the virtuoso himself, in groups of no more than eight, lasting for no more than one hour. Certainly these guests examined the natural history specimens, viewed the works of art, and saw the books and historical artifacts. They were also given an opportunity to examine an exhibit of coins and paper money, to which Du Simitière dedicated an entire section of his museum.[47] This was one of the earliest museum exhibits of coins in America, although the museums of the Library Company of Philadelphia and the American Philosophical Society had probably exhibited coins prior to the 1780s. Unfortunately, no drawings or descriptions have survived to tell us how he organized his collection for display.

We can be certain, however, that Du Simitière discharged one function of a museum, by gathering data about the objects he collected. His papers contain information on numismatics, sometimes apparently scribbled hastily as he heard it, at other times carefully recorded after first being organized. An example of a careful recording is found under the heading "*Observations Sur Les Sauvages*," in which Du Simitière noted the derivation of the words "wampum" and "string wampum" and then recorded the following valuable information:

> Formerly in New York, three black wampum or six white, was a Stuyver. 20 Stuyver was a guilder and a guilder is Six Pences of the present [ca. 1770] New York currency. In 1643 the fathom of wampum was worth four guilders upon Long Island according to De Vries in *His Voyages to New Netherlands.*[48]

American Museum.

THE Subscriber having been induced from several motives, to open his Collection for the inspection of the Gentlemen and Ladies, Strangers in this City, and their Friends, who are desirous to see the Curiosities it contains, thinks it incumbent upon him, to subjoin for their information, a short enumeration of the subjects of which it is composed, collected from most parts of America, the West-Indies, Africa, the East-Indies, and Europe.

NATURAL CURIOSITIES.

MARINE PRODUCTIONS. A very large and complete Collection of the most rare and beautiful Shells, Sea-eggs, Corals, Sea-plants, Fishes, Tortoises, Crabs, Sea-stars, and other curious animal productions of the sea.

LAND PRODUCTIONS. Rare Birds, and parts of Birds and Nests; a variety of Snakes, Lizzards, Bats, Insects, and Worms, the most of them from different parts of the West-Indies.

FOSSILS. Ores of various metals, Platina, and other mineral substances, Agates, Moccos, Jaspers, Cornelian, Onyx, Chrysolites, Crystals, Sparrs, Quartzos, Asbestas, and other curious and rare-figured, pellucid and diversely coloured Pebbles.

PETRIFICATIONS, of various kinds of wood, Plants, Fruits, Reptiles, Insects, Bones, Teeth, and of those subjects that once belonged to the sea; such as Shells, Sea-eggs, Sea-worms, Shark's Teeth, Corals, and Madrepores: As also curious concretions of petrified waters, and stony incrustations over several kinds of bodies, natural and artificial.

Likewise, Fossil substances produced by the eruptions of Volcanos.

BOTANY. A very considerable Collection of the most curious Plants of the West-Indies, together with the several productions of those Plants; such as their Wood, Bark, Fruits, Pods, Kernels, and Seeds, all in the highest preservation.

ARTIFICIAL CURIOSITIES.

Antiquities of the Indians of the West-Indies, and of the North American Indians.

Ornamental Dresses of the modern Indians of North and South-America, with their Weapons and Utensils.

Curious ancient European and East-Indian Weapons; also a valuable curiosity from the Island of Otaheité.

Various Weapons, Musical Instruments and Utensils of the Negroes, from the coast of Guinea, and the West-Indies.

A Collection of curious Paintings in Oil, Crayons, Water-colours, Miniature, Enamel, China, with specimens of the ancient and modern transparent painting on glass, and a curious deception of perspective.

Besides a number of miscellaneous Curiosities of various kinds.

The days of admittance are Tuesday, Thursday, Friday and Saturday, and the hours for each company at Eleven and Twelve o'clock in the forenoon, and at Three, Four and Five o'clock in the afternoon, allowing an hour for each company; which to avoid inconveniency to themselves, he hopes will not exceed six, or at most eight in one sett. By sending for tickets a day or two before, the day and hour that suit the company will be particularly mentioned.

He takes this public opportunity to return his grateful thanks to all those persons who for several years past have from various parts of this Continent contributed to increase his Collection, and hopes he will continue to be favoured with such articles as may fall in their possession, more particularly as he intends his Cabinet to be hereafter the foundation of the first American Museum.

TICKETS to be had in the forenoon of every day, Sundays excepted, at his house in Arch-street, above Fourth-street, at HALF A DOLLAR each.

P. E. DU SIMITIERE.

Philadelphia, June 1, 1782.

PRINTED BY JOHN DUNLAP.

Figure 3

"American Museum" Broadside.
   The June 1, 1782 announcement of the opening of Du Simitière's American Museum does not specifically mention his numismatic collection, but does peg the price of admission at 50 cents. (Courtesy, Library Company of Philadelphia.)

Some of the important information Du Simitière saved was pictorial rather than written. The meticulous drawings of New England, Massachusetts, and Rosa Americana coinage, among others, provide valuable early documentation for these pieces (see figs. 1 and 2). Perhaps the most interesting of these drawings are three views of the celebrated "Higley Coppers." (See fig. 2). Du Simitière's draftsmanship was a bit confused by modern standards, for he transposed the obverses and the reverses, but his renderings were technically very accurate. He illustrated both an early variety of the Higley copper (the 1737 "VALUE ME AS YOU PLEASE"—3 Hammers—"I AM GOOD COPPER") and the last variety (the 1739 "VALUE ME AS YOU PLEASE"—Broad Axe—"J CUT MY WAY THROUGH"). It is fascinating to note that the Higley coppers were elusive even in the 1770s, for the best specimen of the 1737 "THE VALUE OF THREE PENCE"—3 Hammers—"CONNECTICVT" piece he could find was badly worn on the right side of both the obverse and the reverse. Thus Du Simitière's drawings provide mute, but important evidence of the rarity of Higley tokens in better grades, for even though the competition from other collectors was miniscule, Du Simitière could not find a nice specimen.

Du Simitière particularly enjoyed preserving reports of coin hoard discoveries. He recorded some of these stories so excitedly he failed to note all of the facts, or even complete his sentences. One such cryptic passage reads, "I have heard in [October?] 1765 of some silver coins being discovered in the ground about 60 miles [?] country..."[49] The Swiss was usually much more meticulous in his chronicles. For instance, in his annotations of an unnamed book on the history of Jamaica, Du Simitière took pains to accurately describe the hoards he had learned of on that island:

> In June 1761 Mr. Williams of Goshen St. Ann Parish, informed me that, a Mr. King found in Spanish Town about 20 years ago, a jarr full of Copper Coins...In the year 1762 another jarr full of Copper money was dug up on the plantation of Thomas Bontein Esq...In February 1774 being at Leogamme in the Island of Hispaniola, Monsr. Sigonneau Planter presented me with three Spanish copper coins of which a large earthen potful had been found a few years before in one of the cane pieces of his plantation...[50]

These reports were mere hearsay and thus not verifiable. But the Swiss did not mean to judge the merits of such stories. As a museum proprietor, he felt his role was to save these bits of data; he was content to let others squabble over their veracity. In any case, however, it was clear that Du Simitière took his curatorial duties very seriously.

Du Simitière, of course, did more than gather information for his museum,

The Eagle That Is Forgotten

he collected the actual coins as well. In fact, he actively solicited specimens from his far-flung correspondents. Writing to an acquaintance in Virginia, Du Simitière asked for donations of artifacts, "particularly ancient weapons, coins, medals & c. for all these I have proper places alloted in my repository and Some already collected from various parts of the continent."[51] This confirms that Du Simitière aimed to collect coins systematically and widely throughout the British provinces before the Revolution. Du Simitière was fortunate to be among the earliest coin collectors in America, so he had little competition for his prizes. On the other hand, hard money was never plentiful in the provinces, and the crisis of the Revolution exacerbated an already dismal monetary situation. In 1779, in a letter to Governor George Clinton of New York, Du Simitière sounded a lament that coin collectors have echoed ever since: "Coins and medals antient & modern I have a collection of but now a days there become Scarce, notwithstanding I meet with a few now and then."[52]

Indeed Du Simitière did meet with a "few now and then." A 1779 inventory of his numismatic collection revealed 135 separate coins and medals of many nations. Among them were nine New England coins, 13 Rosa Americana pieces, five Virginia coins, and a whopping seven "deer money" pieces [Higley coppers]. Among the coins of the world were three Russian and five Chinese pieces.[53] A visitor to the Swiss's museum would not see a comprehensive overview of either American or world coinage, but he might see a nice introduction to coinage the world over. Considering the premium on hard money during the Revolution, this itself was an amazing achievement, particularly so because it had been fewer than 10 years before that Du Simitière had been forced to surrender 135 valuable silver coins and medals to the estate of John Smith.

Paper Money

Du Simitière did not limit his museum's numismatic collection to coins and medals; he was, in fact, one of America's first collectors of paper money. In a 1783 letter to a patron, Governor George Clinton of New York, Du Simitière stated:

> I have a collection of paper money not only of the colonies but also and particularly of the paper currency emitted [by] Congress and by the different States during the war, but it is imperfect for want of the bills of the State of New York. May I request that you would favour me with some Specimens of its various denominations[?][54]

Du Simitière noted that his collection included the rare, pre-Revolutionary issues of such provinces as Massachusetts, New Hampshire, New Jersey, and North Carolina. It is doubtful if Du Simitière's collection was comprehensive, but it certainly appears to have been extensive. Moreover, the Swiss was constantly attempting to add to it. Less than a month after writing the above letter to Clinton, Du Simitière was courting another patron, one who had apparently sent him some damaged bills for identification:

> ...as to the paper money altho much decayed I could perceive by the dates, that it was struck by the late province of New Hampshire long before the revolution. I wish to have had Some specimens of the paper money of your State emitted during the war, if there has been any Such [,] permit me to request the favour of your procuring some for my collection.[55]

Du Simitière's diligent efforts had previously failed to turn up any bills from New York or New Hampshire, and had led him to wonder if New Hampshire had issued any notes at all. In fact, both states had.[56] This error can hardly obscure Du Simitière's achievement. Operating alone, and with slender resources, he managed to gather a very respectable collection of paper money decades before anyone else became seriously interested in this subject.

The American Museum and Numismatics

The American Museum received numismatic material from a variety of sources. One of its donors was a coin collector of some note himself. Du Simitière's *Memoranda Book* records a gift of "one Heller Scheide muntz 1727...Gift of Rev. Mr. Kunze, Luth. Minister."[57] The Reverend John C. Kunze went on to build a very fine early collection of coins and medals. These eventually were donated to the Museum of the New-York Historical Society, but were later stolen.[58] Du Simitière's association with Kunze, and his earlier contacts with fellow collectors John Smith of Burlington, New Jersey and "Major James" of Philadelphia, suggest that a rudimentary national network of collectors was beginning to form as early as the late 1760s. In any case, the wide and varied list of Du Simitière's numismatic benefactors suggests that several people across America were at least somewhat interested in numismatics before the Revolution.

Du Simitière understood that one mission of a museum is to document its collection. He did so by extracting numismatic literature, and also by making careful pen and ink drawings of his coins. His papers contain well-executed obverse and reverse views of New England coinage, Rosa Americana pieces, Higley coppers, and other coins in his collection, thus providing, in some cases, the earliest known graphic documentation of these pieces. (See figs. 1 and 2.)

The Eagle That Is Forgotten

Figure 4

The "Queen of Pamunkey" Frontlet, Drawn by Du Simitière.
Not a medal, but rather a hand-wrought frontlet, this piece was a forerunner of Indian peace medals. (Courtesy, Library Company of Philadelphia)

The Swiss fulfilled another function of a modern museum: that of providing a reference service for patrons. On February 24, 1779 a Col. Isaac Zane of the "Marlboro' Iron Works" in Virginia, sent Du Simitière, as a gift, a collection of fossils. Zane also sent a drawing of a "medal" he had been offered for purchase, one purportedly given by the English king, Charles II, to the Indian "Queen of Pamunkey" in Virginia. Du Simitière considered the drawing, then sent a reply on March 6 and "recommended him to purchase it at any rate &...that I shall be satisfied to take an exact drawing of it..."[59] Zane apparently accepted Du Simitière's offer, for the Swiss wrote, in May of 1781, that he had added to his collection "a drawing in Indian ink of a silver plate chased & engraved, given by King Charles II to the Queen of Pamunkey in Virginia."[60] (See fig. 4.) The history of this piece is rather obscure. The Pamunkeys were a tribe of Indians living in Virginia as late as 1722.[61] In 1661, the colonists in Virginia passed a law requiring all Indians to wear marks of identification when visiting white outposts. The law specified that "...Silver and plated plaques...be worn by the Indians when visiting the settlements."[62] The Queen of Pamunkey frontlet was thus probably one of these, for it was made during the reign of Charles II (which began in 1660) and it could be attached to clothing by means of five loops on the reverse. This frontlet is, by the very nature of its manufacture, a unique piece. It may be that no similar "medals" exist either, for the "Queen of Pamunkey" frontlet has been conspicuous by its absence at landmark offerings of Indian peace medals.[63]

Finally, Du Simitière's enterprise functioned as a museum in perhaps the most important way. It received valuable gifts *gratis* from supportive donors. A typical entry records, "John Montressor, Esq. Ingenier in Chief of the British Armies in America made me [a] present this day of the following collection of medals of Small bronze, the work of Jean Dassier of Geneva." There follows a list of 17 medals ranging in date from 1617 to 1723, and including such notable subjects as Cardinal Richelieu.[64] As can be inferred from the nationality of this donor, Du Simitière remained neutral during the Revolution, a patriot when the Americans controlled Philadelphia, and a Tory when the British marched in. To Du Simitière, his collection was more important than any national loyalties. The Swiss succeeded in staying on good terms with both sides, and he was able to preserve his collection intact throughout the war.

Du Simitière's Numismatic Legacy

Pierre Eugène Du Simitière left an indelible impression on American numismatics. He was the first to have suggested the use of devices and mottos still employed today for our coinage and paper money. His portrait of George Washington has been used and reused on medals, tokens, and commemorative coins. And, curiously, one of Du Simitière's drawings may have been the

Figure 5

Seal of the Dutch West Indies Company, Drawn by Du Simitière.
An example of Du Simitière's interest in heraldry. (Courtesy, Library Company of Philadelphia.)

Figure 6

Seal of the Province of New Netherlands, 1623-1644, Drawn by Du Simitière.
The crudely executed animal is supposed to be a beaver. (Courtesy, Library Company of Philadelphia.)

The Eagle That Is Forgotten

inspiration for one of the most celebrated frauds in numismatic history, the "Novum Belgium" piece.

The genesis of this peculiar story lies in Du Simitière's interest in heraldry. Among his surviving papers are drawings of seals and coats of arms rendered with careful fidelity to heraldic forms and conventions. Two of these are reproduced as figs. 5 and 6. Fig. 5 is the first seal of the city of New Amsterdam (later New York City) with the insignia WICO [West Indies Company]. Fig. 6 is the seal of New Netherlands (later the province, and still later, the state of New York), for the period 1623-1664. These seals had formed the fourth article of the appendix of Du Simitière's proposed medallic history of the Revolution. It is the latter, the seal of New Netherlands, that became infamous nearly a century after Du Simitière's death.[65]

In 1864, a Yale sophomore named C. Willys Betts sold his collection of colonial coins at public auction. In the catalogue, he admitted to having fabricated some of the pieces, and honestly offered them as counterfeits. One of these fantasy pieces, number eight, was described as follows:

New York piece. Obv. Beaver on Shield (old coat-of-arms of New York under the Dutch government), "Novum Belgium, 1623." Rev.: Crown "Peter Masuit [sic] (first gov.): lead."[66] (See fig. 7)

The piece sold to a "Mr. Nixon" for 40 cents, and was not heard of again until 1877, when Edouard "Ed." Frossard, a New York state coin dealer, excitedly announced, in his new publication Numisma, "Discovery of a Colonial Coin Relating to New Netherlands." Betts' "Novum Belgium" fantasy piece had by now passed, directly or indirectly, from Nixon to Captain Wilson Defendorf, a New York numismatist. The captain submitted the piece to Frossard for examination, and the dealer-publisher, seized by the desire to claim the "...honor of bringing out the coin to the notice of the American collectors..." rushed his description into print.[67]

Frossard was a harsh critic of errors made by others, so there was no shortage of numismatists willing to correct his blunder. The leader of the pack was J.W. Scott, editor of the Coin Collectors' Journal, who exposed Frossard's error, blasted his numismatic judgment, and even abused his English grammar. Frossard at first stuck to his guns (in the January 1878 issue of Numisma); then in the March 1878 issue, admitted his error. He eventually became a respected scholar in the fields of half cents and large cents, but his many detractors never let him forget that he had been bamboozled by an acknowledged forgery.[68]

Figure 7

The "Novum Belgium" Coin.
The celebrated fantasy piece fabricated by C. Willys Betts. (Courtesy, Don Taxay.)

The Eagle That Is Forgotten

It seems clear, both from Betts' own statement, and from design considerations, that the model for the "Novum Belgium" fantasy piece was the seal of the Province of New Netherlands. The central device of a beaver on a shield, although reversed in the Betts version, is clearly borrowed from the seal, as is the bead-topped crown on Betts' reverse. The question then becomes, where did Betts see the seal? As a native of New Haven and a student at Yale, the most likely explanation is the Yale University Library. However, it is possible that Betts, in the course of research, had paid a visit to the Library Company of Philadelphia, and happened upon the "Novi Belgii" piece in the Du Simitière papers. This explanation is admittedly unlikely, but it remains possible in the absence of specific proof to the contrary. This part of Du Simitière's numismatic legacy remains conjectural, and of minor consequence even if true. The remainder, however, is of momentous importance to the future of numismatics in America.

Du Simitière, Consultant on Medals

One of the few triumphs for the rebellious provinces in the opening years of the Revolution came early in March of 1776, when General Washington's seige of Boston forced the British commander, Lord Howe, to evacuate the city. A grateful Congress appointed a committee on March 25, 1776 to prepare a device for a gold medal honoring Washington's achievement. The foremost member of the committee was John Adams, and he turned to Du Simitière as an expert consultant on medals. Adams visited the Swiss in August of 1776 to view his finished drawing of the obverse and sketch of the reverse of the medal. (Both obverse and reverse are shown in fig. 8.) Adams described the obverse in a letter to his wife, Abigail, as being "...Liberty with her spear and pileus, leaning on General Washington. The British Fleet in Boston Harbour, with all their sterns toward the town, the American troops, marching in."[69] As fig. 8 reveals, Adams' description omits only one detail: the exergue is blank. Adams did not, however, describe the reverse; perhaps Du Simitière did not reveal the unfinished sketch to his guest.

The reverse sketch has, as a central device, an all-seeing eye of Providence in a triangle, with glory emanating from it. Underneath is an arm with sword in hand, and the entire central section is enclosed in a circle. Surrounding this circle is a ring of crudely drawn shields, with the name of each state of the new nation written within.

The history of Du Simitière's designs after Adams' visit is rather curious. They were submitted to Congress, and on November 29, 1776, that body authorized payment to Du Simitière in the amount of $32.[70] Congress, however, faced the more pressing business of running a war, so Du Simitière's designs were never executed. It was not until after the Revolution's conclusion,

Figure 8

Obverse Drawing and Reverse Sketch, "Washington Before Boston" Design, Drawn by Du Simitière.

Du Simitière's design for this piece was accepted, but never used. (Courtesy, Library Company of Philadelphia.)

The Eagle That Is Forgotten

in 1786, that Pierre Simon DuVivier, an eminent engraver, executed dies for the "Washington Before Boston" medal, basing his depiction of Washington upon the bust done from life by the French sculptor Jean Antoine Houdon at Mount Vernon in October 1785.[71] Ironically, although Du Simitière's design was left unused and was quickly forgotten, two of its elements, the allegorical rendering of Liberty as a female on the obverse, and the eye of Providence in a triangle radiating glory on the reverse, live on in American numismatics, as will be seen shortly.

Du Simitière, Consultant on the Great Seal of the United States

On the momentous day of July 4, 1776, the Continental Congress created the United States of America by accepting the Declaration of Independence. As their last act of business on that day, Congress also approved the following motion:

> Resolved, That Dr. Franklin, Mr. J. Adams, and Mr. Jefferson be a committee to bring in a device for a seal for the United States of America.[72]

The committee arguably boasted the three best minds in America, but of them, only Jefferson had any knowledge of heraldry, and even his background was not extensive. Adams, however, had worked with Du Simitière on the "Washington Before Boston" medal and Jefferson had consulted with the Swiss on a design for the seal of the state of Virginia.[73]Naturally then, they turned to Philadelphia's leading expert on heraldry, Pierre Eugène Du Simitière. In a letter to his wife, dated August 14, 1776, Adams described Du Simitière's role as a consultant to the committee:

> I am put on a Committee to prepare...Devices for a Great Seal for the confederated States. There is a Gentleman here of French Extraction whose Name is Du simitiere a painter by Profession whose Designs are very ingenious, and his Drawings are well executed. He has been applied to for his advice. I waited on him yesterday, and saw his Sketches.[74]

The sketch Adams saw is reproduced as fig. 9. It consisted of a large shield flanked by two supporters, and surmounted by a crest. Within the shield were six squares symbolizing England, Scotland, Ireland, France, Germany, and the Netherlands, the countries that had peopled the Americas. These six symbols were surrounded by 13 smaller shields representing the 13 new American states. The supporters were the goddess of Liberty on the left, and an American soldier in buckskin on the right. The crest was the eye of Providence in a radiant triangle, its glory extending over the field, past Liberty and the soldier. The motto, unfolding on a banner underneath the shield, read "E Pluribus Unum." There was no reverse. In creating this design, Du Simitière had clearly borrowed the female figure of Liberty and the eye of Providence in a radiant triangle from his "Washington Before Boston" design.

As it happened, each member of the committee had his own pet proposal. The committee's final report, submitted on August 20, 1776, recommended Du Simitière's design for the obverse virtually without alteration; and suggested a combination of Franklin's and Jefferson's plans for the reverse. This proposal was tabled, thus launching a veritable saga of seal making; it took two more committees and nearly six more years before the seal, as we know it today, was finally adopted. Many of Du Simitière's ideas, dating back to his rejected "Washington Before Boston" proposal, survived as elements on the seal as accepted. In the slightly more than two centuries since the seal was given its final form, it has inspired, in whole or in part, the design of dozens of issues of United States coins and medals. So Du Simitière has had an enormous impact, both directly and indirectly, on the future of American numismatics, down to the bills and change in our pockets today.

Du Simitière's Direct Influence on Devices and Mottos

The first of Du Simitière's influences on the future form of American numismatics, the use of a female figure as an allegorical representation of Liberty, was first employed on the rejected "Washington Before Boston" design, then used again on his design for the Great Seal. The idea was certainly not original with Du Simitière, for examples of the use of the female form on coinage as a personification of a nation or as the embodiment of the concept of Liberty date to ancient times. Yet Du Simitière was the first to suggest the representation of Liberty as a goddess for the new nation, and his idea fell on receptive ears. In rapid succession, goddesses of Liberty appeared on the unofficial coppers of Massachusetts (with the "Janus Copper" reverse even labeled "Goddess Liberty"),[75] the Immune Columbia and the Immunis Columbia pieces, Confederatio coppers, the state coinage of Connecticut, New York, and Vermont, and certain private pieces, such as the Auctori Plebis Token (an English Conder Token whose obverse portrait was copied from the Connecticut Draped Bust design), and the Talbot, Allum & Lee cents. Miss Liberty appeared on nearly every United States coin of the 18th and 19th centuries, before being phased out in the middle of the 20th. She is, however, as of this writing, making a small comeback on United States bullion coins.

Figure 9
"Great Seal of the United States" Proposal, Drawn by Du Simitière.
Although this design was rejected, many of its elements were utilized in the accepted form of the Seal. (Courtesy, Library of Congress.)

Another part of Du Simitière's "Washington Before Boston" medal proposal, the eye of Providence in a triangle with glory, was the first part of Du Simitière's design to be accepted as a final element of the Great Seal. A modified version (eye and glory only, no triangle) made a brief appearance from 1783 to 1785 on the Nova Constellatio coppers, the Immune Columbia pieces, and certain Vermont coppers. However, it has had a long and honorable history on the reverse of every one-dollar bill printed since 1928.

The second of Du Simitière's adopted suggestions for the Great Seal, the date in Roman numerals, has also graced the reverse of Federal Reserve Note "ones." In addition, Roman numerals had a brief but glorious history in United States coinage on the MCMVII (1907) Saint-Gaudens high relief double eagle. Again, as of this writing, Roman numerals are being revived on the American eagle gold bullion coins.

Du Simitière's third accepted element for the Great Seal, the form of a shield, has proved nearly as influential upon our nation's coinage as the allegorical figure of Liberty. This traditional heraldic device had a long history on imperial coinage made for America (for example, on the Virginia halfpennies), so one can hardly claim that subsequent coin designers who used shields took inspiration solely from Du Simitière's design. It is fair to say, however, that Du Simitière's idea was the inspiration for the shield on the Great Seal, and several later designers who used shields copied theirs directly from the Great Seal. Among the copies were the Immunis Columbia Shield Reverses, the New Jersey coppers, Indian Head cents after 1859, two-cent pieces, silver three-cent pieces, Shield nickels, Draped Bust and Capped Bust coins, all Liberty Seated coins, Barber halves, most quarter and half eagles, many eagles and double eagles, and assorted territorial gold coins. The shield even made an appearance on the reverse of the Confederate half dollar and several issues from the Philippines. It survives on present-day coinage on the reverse of the Kennedy half dollar.

The fourth element of Du Simitière's design that survived as part of the final form of the Great Seal has exerted truly enormous influence over subsequent designs in American numismatics. Although the motto "E Pluribus Unum" was not Du Simitière's invention, he was the first to suggest it as a motto for America.[76] When it found a place on the Great Seal as finally adopted, it was destined to be used numismatically. Its first appearance came on the 1786 Immunis Columbia piece with Eagle Reverse, and on New Jersey coppers of 1786, 1787, and 1788. In the following year, it made an appearance, as "Unum E Pluribus," on the celebrated Brasher doubloon, and the Excelsior coppers of New York. It is found again on the reverse of the Kentucky tokens attributed to 1792-1794. "E Pluribus Unum" first made an appearance on the federal coinage on the Capped Bust to Right Heraldic Eagle 1795 half eagle. Thus began a long list of coins carrying the phrase; today every circulating coin and the one-dollar bill bear Du Simitière's suggested motto.

Du Simitière's Indirect Influence on Devices and Mottos

Besides Du Simitière's direct legacies for the future appearance of both coinage and paper money, he may have had crucial indirect influences as well. Charles Thomson, a teacher, businessman, politician, and secretary of Congress, in June of 1782 synthesized the recommendations of all three committees formed to suggest designs for the Great Seal, to which he added a few elements of his own. The third committee had decided that an eagle should be one of the devices. Thomson felt that was a good idea, but expanded the concept into a heraldic eagle superimposed on a shield. The eagle-with-a-shield was a device of long standing in European heraldry—the Imperial Arms of Russia, for example, featured a two-headed eagle with a shield on its breast— so it is doubtful that this was solely Thomson's idea. He may have found his inspiration in a book of emblems written by Joachim Camerarius in 1597 that was in the library of Benjamin Franklin.[77] Alternatively, he may have received his idea from his friend, Pierre Eugène Du Simitière.

Thomson knew Du Simitière from the latter's service to several Congressional committees, and both were members of the American Philosophical Society. It seems likely that Thomson shared Du Simitière's interest in coins.[78] In any event, we know that Du Simitière owned several coins from nations that used the eagle-and-shield device on their coinage, specifically Russia, Spain, and the Holy Roman Empire. In his *Memoranda Book*, Du Simitière listed the following coins with eagle motifs in his collection:

> a small [copper piece] II *gute pfer land muntz* 1712.
> reverse a crowned eagle.
> a [small copper piece] III *heller* 1760. reverse, a
> coat of arms in an imperial eagle crowned.
> a 1/8 of a Rixdaller of Leopole, his bust, &
> reverse the imperial a spread eagle, 1760.
> a copper coin of Russia, and imperial eagle, reverse
> an Russian legend, date 1735.
> ¼ Stuber, 1752. *round dortmande Scheide Muntz.*
> reverse an eagle.[79]

It is abundantly clear that Thomson knew Du Simitière, that Thomson had at least some interest in coins, and that Du Simitière's coin collection offered at least five examples of the use of eagles on coinage. Although it cannot be proved, the circumstantial evidence would suggest that Du Simitière was indirectly responsible for the final form of the eagle on the Great Seal, and thus on later coinage designs. An eagle had first appeared on American coinage on the obscure (and today, very rare) "New Yorke" token issued sometime between 1664 and 1710.[80] The adoption of the Great Seal in 1782, however, led to a veritable population explosion of eagles on American coins. The 1786 Immunis Columbia with Eagle Reverse was the first, and it was soon joined by Massachusetts half cents and cents, the Brasher doubloon, the Excelsior coppers of New York as well as various other New York issues, Mott tokens, and several Washington pieces. The first United States Mint coin, the 1792 half disme, had an eagle on the reverse, and other United States issues too numerous to name were to follow. Today, by law, all coins of a denomination greater than 10 cents must carry an eagle on the reverse. Clearly, the influence of Charles Thomson, and perhaps indirectly, the influence of Pierre Eugène Du Simitière, is still being felt today on United States coinage.[81]

Du Simitière and Washington Pieces

Du Simitière's legacy pervades all types of United States coinage, but it is especially concentrated in one series: Washington pieces. The reason for this is quite simple. The Revolutionary era predated the age of practical photography by nearly 70 years. Painted portraits were the only real means available to preserve a person's likeness, but if that person happened to be famous, a handful of original portraits, taken from life, would never be enough to satisfy the people's curiosity to see his face. In such a case, an artist could copy a portrait onto stone in order to make cheap engraved reproductions of the oil painting. This was precisely the situation in 1779. Nearly four years after the outbreak of the Revolution, most Europeans, and even a majority of Americans, had never seen a good likeness of George Washington, and there was a tremendous desire to behold the features of the man who was defying the mighty British Crown.

This demand awakened the entrepreneur in Du Simitière, and he asked his friend John Jay, the president of Congress, to arrange a sitting by the busy general. The honorable Mr. Jay was successful, for, under the date of "1779, Feb. 1" in his *Common Place Book*, Du Simitière recorded:

> ...a drawing in black lead of a likeness in profil of his excellency general Washington, form of a medal for my collection. N.B. The general at the request of the Hon. Mr. Jay, President of Congress, came with him to my house this morning & condescended with great good nature to Sit about 3/4 of an hour for the above likeness having little time to Spare, being the last day of his stay in town.[82]

These 45 minutes were destined to have a lasting impact on American numismatics. Du Simitière was anxious to turn his good fortune into profit, so he conceived an ambitious plan to draw a series of American leaders, send the drawings to France to be engraved, then sell the resulting sets to people both in America and abroad. The set, which totaled 14 names, among them many still familiar today, was mostly assembled in 1779.[83] By September 16, 1779, he delivered the completed portraits to the French Minister to the United States, Conrad Alexander Gerard, whom he had enlisted to assure that the portraits would reach France safely.[84] In gratitude, Du Simitière made Monsieur Gerard the 15th hero in the series; it appears, however, that Gerard's portrait was never published as an engraving, nor was that of another of Du Simitière's subjects, Thomas Mifflin.[85]

Du Simitière's luck with these portraits was disastrous. His drawings did make it to Paris, where the celebrated engraver Bénoit Louis Prévost executed them in two groups, the first of six, the second of seven. The authorized French edition then suffered a series of calamities; a number were captured at sea by the British and still others were damaged in transit. It was not until 1782 that fragmentary sets reached America, and less than a year later, two pirated English editions came out within five days of each other. Du Simitière naturally received no royalties from the pirated editions, so his financial condition worsened again.[86]

The public on both sides of the water took a great liking to Du Simitière's rendering of Washington (See fig. 10). Du Simitière in fact, credited this picture with selling the entire set. He wrote, "I could have sold many prints of our commander in chief [separately]...I believe some purchased a whole sett principal on account of that likeness."[87] The portrait, although technically competent, is not particularly inspired. It depicts Washington in profile, facing left, in full uniform, with his hair drawn into a queue in back. As compared to the "standard" portrait of Washington (the Jean Antoine Houdon bust, based on the life mask taken at Mount Vernon in October of 1785, on which the Washington quarter portrait is based), Du Simitière's depiction is fleshier, with a fatter neck and a larger nose. Nevertheless, in 1782, authentic images of Washington were at such a premium that even a somewhat indifferent portrait was eagerly embraced by coiners.

There is widespread agreement that this portrait has been perpetuated on a number of Washington pieces; there is, however, nothing close to unanimous agreement as to which pieces. The starting point has to be William S. Baker's *Medallic Portraits of Washington*, first published in 1885. Baker, who was the foremost expert of his time on images of Washington, held some erroneous notions about Du Simitière, but he was absolutely correct in recognizing the Swiss as an important influence on Washington pieces.[88] Baker judged sever-

Drawn from the life by Du Simitier *in Philadelphia.* *Engraved by* B.L. Prevost *at Paris.*

Figure 10
George Washington, Engraving After Original Drawing by Du Simitière.
Du Simitière's original sketch, done in 1779, became the basis for several Washington pieces.
(Courtesy, Library Company of Philadelphia)

al obverse portraits on Washington pieces to be copies of the Du Simitière engraving, 24 varieties to be precise. Yet when Russell Rulau and George Fuld revised the Baker reference in 1985, they were far more conservative, attributing only five obverse varieties as copies of the Du Simitière engraving.[89] To add to the confusion, Walter Breen and Anthony Swiatek in their *Encyclopedia of United States Silver and Gold Commemorative Coins,* attributed a commemorative coin (created after Baker's death), to the Du Simitière portrait, while Rulau and Fuld credit Charles Barber, the chief engraver of the United States Mint, for this piece.[90]

Which of these versions is closer to being correct? It seems logical to begin with the pieces on which there is unanimous agreement. These are Baker 277 and 278 (the "Cincinnatus of America" medals); Baker 288 (the "General Grand Master" Masonic medals); Baker 352 (the "Industry Produces Wealth" medal); and Baker 529 (the "John K. Curtis Store Card").

Baker was rather liberal in tracing Du Simitière's influence. He attributed to the Swiss's portrait of Washington the following obverses: Baker 15 (Large Eagle cent); Baker 16 (Small Eagle cent); Baker 17 (Liverpool halfpenny); Baker 18 (Ship halfpenny); Baker 20, 21 and 23-25 (Washington half dollars); Baker 22 (Washington cent); Baker 29 (Grate cent); Baker 30 and 31 (Liberty and Security pieces); Baker 34 and 35 (North Wales tokens); and Baker 59 and 60 ("General of the American Armies" medals). In addition, Baker felt that his number 26 (the Fonrobert copy of the Washington half dollar) was probably a copy of number 24.

Actually, the wide discrepancy between Baker and Rulau and Fuld is not so insurmountable as it seems, for it stems largely from different criteria of selection. Rulau and Fuld chose a rigorous standard of proof, by which the bust on the coin had to be a virtual twin of the original Du Simitière engraving. Baker, on the other hand, used a looser standard, by which the bust on the coin, if it matched the Du Simitière engraving closely, but not precisely, was assigned to the Swiss. As Baker put it, "The heads on these pieces bear a close resemblance to the print, which must have furnished the models for their execution."[91] To put this difference into more concise terms, Rulau and Fuld demanded that the coin exhibit a first-generation copy of the Du Simitière engraving, while Baker was willing to accept a second- or third-generation copy.

Both positions have their advantages and disadvantages. The conservative approach of Rulau and Fuld is probably 100% accurate as far as it goes, but it undoubtedly excludes several pieces which owe a great deal of their design inspiration to Du Simitière. Baker's liberal approach probably credits nearly every piece that Du Simitière influenced, but may also include a few to which he made no contribution. From a "scientific" point of view, the former approach is the best, for it is more verifiable, but from an aesthetic standpoint, one can hardly deny an artist's influence simply because the work has been copied more than once.

Bearing this in mind, Baker is probably closer to the truth. Du Simitière's Washington engraving was widely copied at the time, appearing on items as diverse as Wedgwood tea caddies and mirrored doorknobs.[92] It is not at all unlikely that the portraits on some Washington pieces were lifted from such copies, and thus may vary significantly from the original. In some cases, such as the Large and Small Eagle cents (Baker 15 and 16), the changes are so small that they are hardly worth mentioning. In others, such as the Grate cent, (Baker 29) the changes are significant, and it is a matter of aesthetic judgment to attribute the piece to Du Simitière at all. It is probably safe to say then, that Du Simitière's engraving of Washington served as a direct model for at least five Washington pieces, and probably as the original source for 15 to 19 more.[93] Thus the 45 minutes that Washington spent with Du Simitière on a cold winter's day in 1779 cast a long shadow over the future of American numismatics.

Du Simitière's Death and the Sale of the American Museum

Du Simitière had opened the American Museum in April of 1782, but it never became a paying proposition. By September of that year, he complained to Monsieur Gerard, the French minister, that business was poor and that "I find it exceedingly difficult to keep together what I have been collecting for a great number of years..."[94] As his financial situation deteriorated, Du Simitière could have reduced costs by curtailing his collecting activities, or raised money by selling part of his collection. As his letter to Gerard suggests, however, the Swiss simply could not bear to part with the treasures it had taken him a lifetime to collect. Du Simitière instead continued to add artifacts to his museum, and his finances continued to sag.

In March of 1783, disaster struck. An illness forced the amputation of a joint from a finger on his left hand. The operation, performed without benefit of anesthetic, left Du Simitière in terrible pain for weeks thereafter. He was unable to open his museum for nearly a month, and he never fully regained his artistic ability. With his two sources of income thus disrupted, Du Simitière's financial situation became critical. By the end of 1783, his health began to fail, and he abruptly stopped writing letters and keeping records. In a desperate attempt to make ends meet, he began, in 1783, to take on drawing pupils. One of them was Thomas Jefferson's daughter, Martha, and a number of Jefferson's letters drew a pathetic picture of a desperate man trying to squeeze his clients for every cent in order to stay alive.[95] Desperate though he had become, Du Simitière could not bring himself to part with his collection, or even part of it. When he died, in October of 1784 (the date is unclear: either the 10th or the 22nd), his museum was still intact. Of Du Simitière it can truly be said that he would rather collect than eat, for the generally accepted cause of his death was starvation.[96]

Du Simitière left no heirs. Matthew Clarkson (who later became the mayor of Philadelphia) and the bookseller Ebenezer Hazard were appointed executors. Although Hazard later claimed he had accepted the post "with a view to prevent his museum from being scattered," the bookseller and his partner worked with dispatch to do just the opposite.[97] On March 19, 1785, the contents of the American Museum, comprising 36 large lots, were sold at public auction in Philadelphia. Among them were 18 lots of books, nine of drawings and prints, and five of "curiosities." Two lots, numbers 19 and 36, make this sale of special interest to numismatists.

According to the "bible" of coin sales, Attinelli's *Numisgraphics*, "What is possibly the 'first' announcement of a 'Public Coin Sale' in this country," came from the Salem *Gazette* of June 6, 1828, announcing the sale of the effects of Benjamin Watkin, deceased, on June 12 and 13, 1828.[98] Yet the Du Simitière sale, held 43 years earlier, had, as Lot 19, "A mahogany Cabinet containing ancient and modern Gold, Silver, and Copper Coins and Medals; among which are some very curious Bronzes"; and Lot 36, "A collection of Parchment and Paper Money."[99] (See fig. 11.) As of this writing, this modest broadside represents the oldest known public auction of coins in America.

We know the disposition of at least part of Du Simitière's collection. Many of the books, including some of the numismatic works, went to the Library Company of Philadelphia, where they remain today. As for his coins and paper money, George Frederick Kolbe has suggested that the Philadelphia painter Charles Willson Peale secured a portion of Du Simitière's coins for his own Philadelphia museum.[100] This is conceivable, for in 1787, Ebenezer Hazard donated "sundry articles" to Peale's Museum, which were possibly unsold remainders from Du Simitière's American Museum. Unfortunately, Peale, in his thank you letter to Hazard, did not identify the objects he had received.[101] Peale's Museum did have a substantial numismatic collection, but none of it can be positively pedigreed to Du Simitière. A more promising and intriguing lead comes from a letter Hazard wrote to Thomas Bradford on February 17, 1790: "Sir, I have recd. yours respecting DuSimitiere, and have written to Mr. Clarkson on the subject. He has both the papers and money belonging to that estate."[102] In using the term "money," was Hazard referring to the receipts of the sale, or to Du Simitière's numismatic collection? It seems

Figure 11

Broadside of Sale, 1785, for Du Simitière's American Museum.
Lots 19 and 36 make this the oldest known public auction sale of coins and paper money held in America. (Courtesy, Library Company of Philadelphia.)

reasonable that the proceeds from the sale would have been disbursed by 1790, since the auction had been held nearly five years previously. If so, it appears that Clarkson may have purchased the coins. In that case, Clarkson would have been perhaps the first person in America to buy coins at public auction. There is not so much as a clue as to the identity of the purchaser of Lot 36, Du Simitière's paper money.

We can be almost certain that Clarkson did purchase Lot 19, Du Simitière's coins. The "smoking gun" is found in an advertisement for the auction of Clarkson's estate, which appeared in the October 29, 1800 issue of *Poulson's American Daily Advertiser.* The advertisement describes the coin collection in almost exactly the same words in which it was described as Lot 19 in the Du Simitière sale (See fig. 12). Here then was possibly the second public auction of coins in America. It is indeed unfortunate that no records were kept as to the identity of the coins' purchaser at the Clarkson sale.[103]

Du Simitière's Place in Numismatic History

Du Simitière's remarkable numismatic contributions have not been recognized during the more than two centuries since his death, a fate they do not deserve. Du Simitière was one of America's first true collectors of numismatic material and paper money. He aspired to be one of America's first numismatic authors, and he succeeded in forming one of the earliest numismatic collections in an American museum. He unwillingly was responsible for the earliest known American sale of coins at fixed prices, and the earliest known American auction of coins and paper money. Finally, his suggestions for the design of the Great Seal of the United States have cast an enormous shadow over the subsequent history of American numismatic and paper money design. In fact, it is not too much to say that Du Simitière has been one of the most important influences on the design of American coinage.

It is appropriate to close, as we began, by quoting Charles Willson Peale. In his autobiography, written shortly before his death in 1826, Peale remembered:

> a French artist Mr. Dusimetere painted miniature pictures...He also collected some few articles of antiquity with a hope of forming a Museum...He had a few coins, perhaps they were the most valuable part of his collection.[104]

Peale, as was his wont, downplayed the numbers and the significance of his predecessor's collections. Yet the truth is always revealed, later if not sooner. Even the critical Mr. Peale had to admit that Du Simitière's coins were "valuable." In truth they were more than monetarily precious; they were historical-

To be fold by public auction,

At **No. 109**, Arch ftreet, (being the late dwelling
houfe of Matthew Clarkfon, Efq. deceafed,) on
Thurfday next the 30th inft. at 9 o'clock, A.M.
A variety of houfhold and kitchen Furniture.

Silver and plated ware, a good eight day clock,
a very curious bedftead peculiarly conftructed for
the ufe of fick perfons, an iron cheft, and a valuable cabinet, containing filver and copper coin,
medals, &c. fome of which are very ancient.

Figure 12

Advertisement of Sale for Matthew Clarkson's Estate.
This advertisement appeared in *Poulson's American Daily Advertiser* on October 29, 1800.
Note that the language used to describe the coins is nearly identical to that of Lot 19 in
the Du Simitière sale. Thus Thursday October 30, 1800 may be the date of the second auction of coins in America. (Courtesy, Library Company of Philadelphia.)

The Eagle That Is Forgotten

ly priceless. Whatever their monetary value might have been, their worth to the numismatic historian is far greater. For his love for coins made Pierre Eugène Du Simitière the first great figure in American numismatics. After two centuries of undeserved obscurity, "The Eagle That is Forgotten" can now take his rightful place as a founding father of American numismatics.

APPENDIX

Pieces de   or   argt   cuivre   Pieces d   or   argent   cuivre

Pieces de	or	argt	cuivre		Pieces d	or	argent	cuivre
Savoye			1.	France très ancienne		1	
Bâle			3.	divers			4
Berne			1.	colonies francs.			1
Soleure			1.	mine de france			1
Zurich			1.	Milan		2 . 1	
Geneve		5. 5.		Pape Sede vacante 1555		1	
Strasbourg			2.	divers		2 .	
Wurtzbourg			1.	Lucques		1	
Saltz bourg			1.	Parme	1 .		
Baviere			1.	Venise	2 .	1 .	
Pieces d'hongrie			2.	Turquie	1 .	3 .	
hanover		1 . 1.		Pruse		4.	
colmar		1 .		Hambourg		2 .	
Cleves			3.	Saxe		1 .	
Wirtemberg			4.	archid. Leopold	1	1.	
Hesse Darmstad			2.	Cologne		1 .	
Bremen			2.	Nuremberg		1 .	
hollande			1.	comte mansfeld 1665		1 .	
utrecht			2.	Ferdin. II. Emp. 1623		1 .	
geldres		2 . 2.		Ferdin. III. Emp. 1656		1 .	
groningue		1.		Angleterre Henri VI.		1 .	
Zeelande		2 . 1.		Henri VII.		1 .	
Frise		1.		Edward VI.		1 .	
Overissel		1.		Phil. & Mary.		1 .	
Pays bas autrichiens		5 . 6.		Elizab.	1 .	2 .	
Lille du Marechal de Boufflers		1.		Charl I		3 .	
Suede		1 . 4.		Charl. II	2 .	6 . 2 .	
...		1.		Jaques II	1.	3 . 2 .	
Danemarck		14 .		Willi. & Mary	1.	3 . 1 .	
Russie		1.		William III		4 . 2 .	
Prusse		1 . 3.		Anne	1 .	5 .	
Chine		1.		George I		2 . 1 .	
Portugal		5 .		George II		3 . 2 .	
Espagne ferdinand & isabella	1 .	1.		Oliv. Cromwell		1 .	
divers		16 . 3.		William III		2 .	
France Henri 4		2.		Irlande Charl II		3 .	
Louis 13		1 . 1.		George I		3 .	
Louis 14		8 . 2.		George II		2 .	
Louis 15		9 . 2.		Voce Populi		2	
				Colon. Amer.		2	
				New Engl. Isle of Man		2 . 1	

Du Simitière's Undated Coin Inventory, "Old Coins. Collection of Old Coins from Different Countries" *Scraps*, No. 39, HSP

Catalogue des medailles Romaines
dans ma collection

moyen bronze

№ 1. a. Imp. Caip. Augusti & agrippa. aversi. p. col. nem. crocodilus palmæ alligatus.

2. a. Ti. Cæsar. august. Imperat. VII. p. Rom et aug. ara cum duab. victor

grand bronze

3 a. a. nerva Traiano. aug. germ. Dac. P.M. p. S. P. Q. R. opt. prin.

3. b. a. nerva Traian. aug. p. S.C.

4. a. Hadrianus augustus. Cap. Laur. p. Neptunus Stans. d. tridentem S. pedem prora imposito

5. a. Sabina augusta p. mulier Stans.

6. a. Antoninus aug. p. mulier Stans. SC

7. a. Faustina augusta p. figura Stans.

Petit bronze

8. a. Imper. Claudius. aug. p. Victoria aug.

9. a. a. Divo Claudio. p. Consecratio. ara cum igne.

9. b. a. Divo Claudio. p. consecratio. ara

9. c. a. Divo Claudio. p. consecratio. aquila

10. a. Imp. Constantinus nous. p. figura

11. a. D.n. magnentius p. f. aug. p. Eques Ke. gloria ....mane...

12. a. Gallien.. p. . cerva

13. a. Imp. Tetricus. pl. aug. p. virtus augg. fig. Stans

14. a. D.n. valentinianus aug. p. fama. vel victoria alata. Securitas .....

14. a. a. Idem .... p. miles cum captivis

14. c. a. Idem .... p. figura hastam tenens Ke.

15. a. urbs Roma. fig. mul. p. fratres cum Lupa.

argent.

16. a. Caput . denarius consularis... b. victoria cum tropheo

17. a. Tit. Cæsar. Divi. aug. f. augustus. p. Pontif. maxim. fig. mul. Sed. d. hastam. S. ramum.

or

18. a. D.n. valentinianus. Iun. P. f. aug. p. victoria coronans Lutatia & velati. victoria aug.

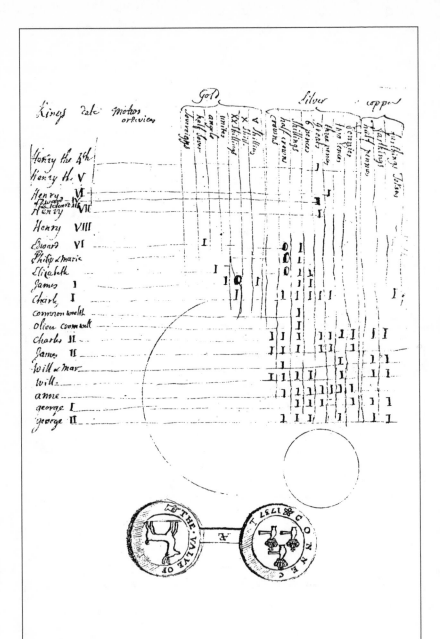

Du Simitière's Undated Coin Inventory, Untitled. A listing of British coins by metal and by sovereign depicted. At bottom, a sketch of a Higley copper. *Scraps*, #54, HSP

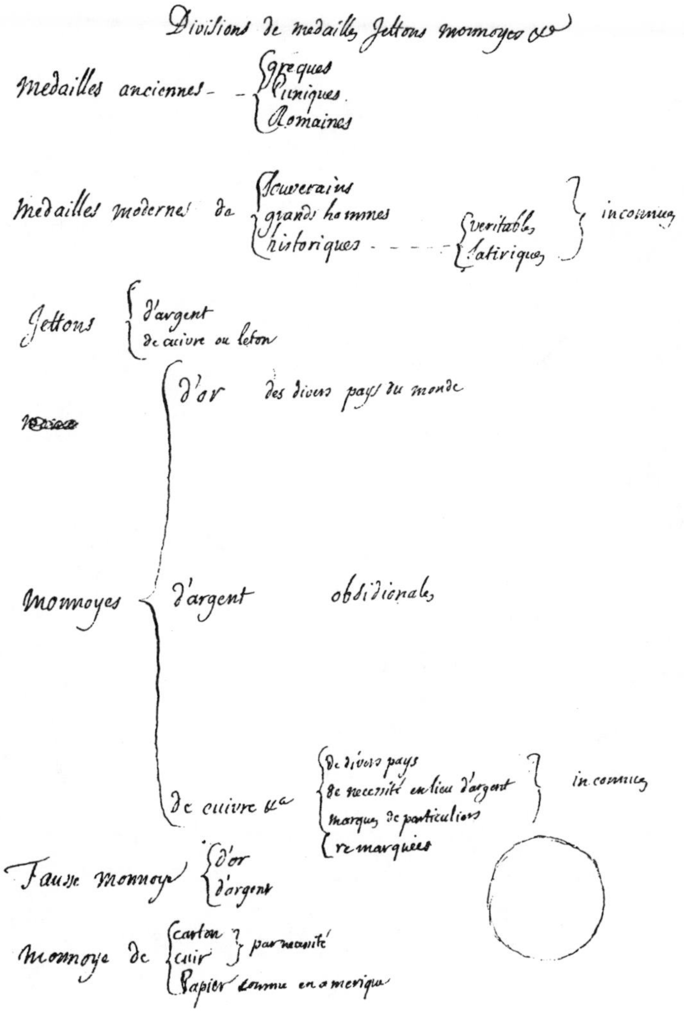

Divisions de medailles, Jettons monnoyes &c

Medailles anciennes _
{ greques
{ uniques.
{ Romaines

Medailles modernes de
{ Souverains
{ grands hommes
{ historiques - - - - -
{ veritables
{ satiriques
} inconnues

Jettons
{ d'argent
{ de cuivre ou leton

Monnoyes {
d'or   des divers pays du monde

d'argent   obsidionales

de cuivre &c
{ De divers pays
{ de necessité en lieu d'argent
{ marques de particuliers
{ remarquées
} inconnues

Fausse monnoye
{ d'or
{ d'argent

monnoye de
{ carton }
{ cuir } par necessité
{ Papier comme en amerique

Du Simitière's Undated Numismatic Classification, "Divisions of Medals, Jetons, Monnoyes & C." Scraps, #54, HSP

FOOTNOTES

1 Charles Willson Peale to Rembrandt Peale, October 28, 1812. Peale-Sellers Papers, *Letterbook 12*, American Philosophical Society.

2 Charles Willson Peale, 1826 *Autobiography*, p. 99. Peale-Sellers Papers, American Philosophical Society. Peale was no stranger to numismatics. His Philadelphia Museum contained a substantial coin collection, as did the Baltimore Museum directed by his son, Rembrandt, and later by his son, Rubens, as did the New York Museum also run by Rubens. Both the Philadelphia Museum and the New York Museum struck admission tokens which survive today. The Philadelphia Museum struck at least two different types of tokens. The first type, Rulau Pa-398 (See Bowers and Merena's sale of the *Four Memorable Collections*, September 9-11, 1985, Lot 3004 and also Bowers and Merena's sale of *The Collection of Julian Leidman*, April 12, 1986, Lot 4735) featured Charles Willson Peale on the obverse and the words "Admit the Bearer" within a wreath on the reverse. The work of Christian Gobrecht (its obverse is dated "1784," but this refers to the founding of the Museum), it is attributed to 1821. The second type, Julian UN-22, (See Bowers and Ruddy's *The Garrett Collection Sales IV*, October 1-2, 1980, Lot 1972), also Gobrecht's work, has an identical obverse, but has hand-engraved names on the reverse in place of "Admit the Bearer." The New York Museum Token (see Bowers and Merena's *Four Memorable Collections*, Lot 3003), has a helmeted female bust on the obverse and "Admit the Bearer" on the reverse. These were in use from approximately 1825 to 1841. A third Peale son, Titian, drew the designs upon which Christian Gobrecht based the "Liberty Seated" and the "Flying Eagle" motifs for coinage. (See Don Taxay, *The U.S. Mint and Coinage* [New York: Arco Publishing Co., Inc., 1966], pp. 170-76.) A fourth Peale son, Franklin, was for many years the chief coiner of the United States Mint in Philadelphia. To Franklin belongs the credit for modernizing much of the Mint's machinery; to him also belongs the opprobrium of misusing his position for personal gain and being forced to resign under fire. See Taxay, *The U.S. Mint and Coinage*, pp. 149-69; 177-91.

3 Du Simitière lived in New York (1763-64); Charleston (1764-65); Philadelphia (1765-67); Boston (1767-68); Newport (1768); New York (1768-70); Burlington, New Jersey (1770); Philadelphia (1770-72); the West Indies (1772-73); Philadelphia (1773); the West Indies (1773-74); and finally in 1774, he settled permanently in Philadelphia.

4 This may be freely translated as "On the System of Counting and Coining in the Windward and Leeward Isles." By "Isles du Vent," Du Simitière meant the islands of St. Christopher, Antigua, Montserrat, Nevis, Barbados, St. Eustatius, St. Martin, Saba, Martinique, Guadeloupe, Granada, St. Lucia, St. Vincent, Marie-Galante, and Saint-Barthelemy. By "Isles Sous le Vent," he meant Hispaniola, Cuba, Jamaica, Puerto Rico, and Curacao.

5 Pierre Eugène Du Simitière, "Des Manières de Compteu et des Monnoyer des Isles du Vent et Sous le Vent," *Pierre Eugène Du Simitière Papers*, Volume VI, Item 2, 968. F.2, Library Company of Philadelphia.

6 Du Simitière met Smith sometime before November 21, 1766, the date of their earliest surviving correspondence. It is highly unlikely their introduction would have occurred when Du Simitière was in Charleston from 1764 to 1765, so their acquaintance must have begun with a meeting while the Swiss was living in New York (1763-64), or, more likely, while Du Simitière was in Philadelphia from 1765 to 1767. Smith lived in Burlington, obviously Burlington, New Jersey rather than Burlington, Vermont since Burlington, New Jersey is only a few miles from Philadelphia.

7 Du Simitière to William Dillwyn, April 7, 1771. Society Miscellaneous Collections, *Photostats of Autographed Letters Signed*, Historical Society of Pennsylvania.

8 Du Simitière to Evert Bancker, March 31, 1771. *MSS Collection,* American Philosophical Society.

9 Du Simitière to John Smith, Esq., November 21, 1766. *Watson's Annals,* p. 306, Historical Society of Pennsylvania.

10 Du Simitière, *Scraps,* No. 32, Historical Society of Pennsylvania.

11 Du Simitière to John Smith, August 6, 1767. *Etting Collection,* Historical Society of Pennsylvania.

12 Du Simitière to William Dillwyn, April 7, 1771, previously cited.

13 "Catalogue of Medals and Coins of Silver in the Possession of the honble. John Smith Esq. at Burlington." Undated, but 1769. Society Miscellaneous Collections, *Photostats of Autographed Letters Signed,* Historical Society of Pennsylvania. The three-page catalogue reveals that all 135 pieces were silver strikings, representing 21 nations stretching across Europe from Portugal to Russia, and ranging in date from 1605 to 1764. A partial listing of these coins may be found in Harrold E. Gillingham, "An 18th Century Coin Collection," *The Numismatist* 47 (November 1934), pp. 723-24. One of the more interesting pieces in the collection was a 1745 half crown of George II with "LIMA" stamped under the bust. These coins were issued to commemorate the capture of booty from Spain, but two different British naval expeditions are given the credit, depending on which source one consults. See Leon T. Lindheim, *Facts and Fictions About Coins* (Cleveland: World Publishing Company, 1967), pp. 86-87.

14 Du Simitière to Evert Bancker, March 31, 1771, previously cited.

15 Du Simitière to William Dillwyn, April 7, 1771, previously cited.

16 William Dillwyn, notation on back of catalogue of coins belonging to Pierre Eugène Du Simitière, attached to letter of Du Simitière to Dillwyn, April 7, 1771, previously cited.

17 For more information on the Richardsons and the 1793 Indian Peace Medal, see Bowers and Merena's *Sale of the Virgil M. Brand Collection, Part II,* June 18-19, 1984, pp. 48-55. The 1793 "George Washington President" medal engraved by Joseph Richardson, Jr., described as Extremely Fine, appeared as Lot 961.

18 William Dillwyn, notation on back of catalogue, previously cited.

19 Harrold Gillingham, in his aforementioned article, credits the elder Richardson with another numismatic achievement, saying, "It was he who struck the medal for the 'Friendly Association for Preserving Peace with the Indians by Pacific Measures.' " [Betts 401]. See Gillingham, *An 18th Century Coin Collection,* pp. 723-24.

20 See Emmanuel Joseph Attinelli, *Numisgraphics* (New York: Published by the author, 1876.) Reprint edition, *A Bibliography of American Numismatic Auction Catalogues, 1828-1875.* (Lawrence, Massachusetts: Quarterman Publications Inc., 1976.) Attinelli was unable to find any sales of coins before 1828. See pp. 5-6.

21 Harrold Gillingham speculated that the buyer was indeed the William Logan who was James Logan's grandson, but his efforts to confirm his hunch were unsuccessful. See Gillingham, *An Eighteenth Century Coin Collection,* p. 723. For the story of the Smith-Logan family connections, see "John Smith" in *The National Cyclopedia of American Biography,* Vol. 13 (New York: James T. White & Co., 1906), p. 582.

22 Eric P. Newman, in his ground breaking study, *The Secret of the Good Samaritan Shilling (Numismatic Notes and Monographs* No. 142; New York: The American Numismatic Society, 1959), revealed the numismatic activities of Rev. Andrew Eliot (1718-1778). Eliot, the Pastor of Boston's celebrated Old North Church, possessed in 1767 a wide-ranging collection of New England coinage, including many duplicates. The author wishes to thank Eric P. Newman for research help on this topic.

23 Du Simitière, *Scraps*, No. 32, previously cited. All of Du Simitière's dated coin lists are gathered together under this heading.

24 Du Simitière, *Scraps*, No. 54 (British Coins); *Scraps*, No. 39 (Ancient Coins); *Scraps*, No. 2 (Roman Medals); *Scraps*, No. 40 (Catalogue of Ancient and Modern Gold Medals); Historical Society of Pennsylvania. The author is grateful to Michael Hodder of Bowers and Merena Galleries for his evaluation of the significance of the coins in Du Simitière's lists.

25 Du Simitière, *Scraps*, No. 96, "List of Curiosities To Be Found in Philadelphia," Historical Society of Pennsylvania.

26 Paul Ginsberg Sifton, *Pierre Eugène Du Simitière (1737-1784): Collector in Revolutionary America*, Ph.D. dissertation, University of Pennsylvania, 1960, p. 414, note 37. Du Simitière purchased this book from the estate of Col. William Byrd II (1674-1744) who amassed a library of four thousand volumes in Westover, Virginia. The book now resides in the collection of the Library Company of Philadelphia.

27 Du Simitière, *Scraps*, No. 96, previously cited. "Fo." is an abbreviation for "Folio" and "fig." means the book was illustrated.

28 Du Simitière, "COINS: Remarks on Irish Coins." *Common Place Book*, Library of Congress.

29 Du Simitière, "COINS: Remarks on English Coins." *Common Place Book*, Library of Congress.

30 Du Simitière, "American Coins," Volume IX, Item 30, Library Company of Philadelphia.

31 Ibid. Du Simitière may have read this in a book in his collection, *Historie der Boeraniers... Van America* by Alexandre Olivier Exquemelin, published in Amsterdam in 1700. This book now belongs to the Library Company of Philadelphia.

32 Ibid. Du Simitière had a sharp numismatic eye, for in these same notes he states that "there is a great variety of dies" among the New England coinage.

33 Ibid. The author has been unable to locate the "prints" that Du Simitière mentions. See also Leake, *Historical Account of English Money*, 2nd ed., p. 349. For the peculiar story of the Pembroke Collection coins, see Newman, *The Secret of the Good Samaritan Shilling*, pp. 3-6. The author wishes to thank Eric P. Newman for research help on this subject.

34 Ibid.

35 Ibid.

36 See Sylvester Sage Crosby, *The Early Coins of America* (Boston: Published by the author, 1875; Reprint edition, Lawrence, Massachussetts: Quarterman Publications, 1983), p. 74. According to Crosby, this mistaken notion sprang from the illustration of such a spurious "penny" in Folkes' *Tables of English Silver and Gold Coins*. Du Simitière probably used the edition reprinted in London by the Society of Antiquaries in 1763. No such "pennies" were ever minted.

37 Du Simitière, "American Coins," previously cited. Crosby provided an illustration of the "Good Samaritan Shilling" (the Charles I. Bushnell Collection specimen) and speculated it was a pattern piece. See Crosby, *The Early Coins of America*, p. 68. This coin was purchased by Lorin Parmelee in the Chapman Brothers' 1882 sale of the Bushnell Collection, for the huge sum of $650. Not until 1959 did the brilliant detective work of Eric P. Newman prove the coin to be a fraud. See Newman, "The Secret of the Good Samaritan Shilling" (New York: The American

Numismatic Society, 1959). Du Simitière learned of the Good Samaritan Shilling from an illustration on p. 91 of the Folkes book (see note 36 above).

38 Ibid. Du Simitière here referred to the American Plantations Token which featured James II of England on the reverse. These token farthings, struck in tin, were supposed to pass at the ratio of 24 to the Spanish Real.

39 Ibid.

40 Ibid.

41 While the Half Pennies may not have been officially "admitted," they were not, as the passage implies, rejected. The standard source for information on the Virginia coinage is Eric P. Newman, *Coinage for Colonial Virginia* (New York: American Numismatic Society, 1956). Newman asserts many of the Virginia pieces are found well worn, and others have been excavated, along with other contemporary coins, from archaeological digs. Du Simitière was not far wrong, however, for many were hoarded, including a keg of thousands of coins once belonging to Col. Mendes Cohen. For the best recent offering of these pieces, see Bowers and Ruddy's *The Garrett Collection Sales*, Sale 3, Lots 1281-1294. Du Simitière's source may have been Thomas Jefferson, for in his writings on the subject of coinage in Virginia, he erroneously stated "In Virginia...we have never yet been able to introduce a copper coin at all." Thomas Jefferson, "Notes on the Establishment of a Money Unit, and of a Coinage for the United States" (1784) in Phillip S. Foner, ed. *Basic Writings of Thomas Jefferson* (New York: Willey Book Company, 1944), p. 202. Jefferson and Du Simitière were acquaintances by 1775.

42 Du Simitière, "Monnoye. Money, Coins, Origine de la Monnoye." *Common Place Book*, 1775-1784, Library of Congress. The earliest known book published in America on numismatics-related topics was *A Modest Inquiry into the Nature and Necessity of a Paper-Currency*, written and published by Benjamin Franklin in 1729. Only three copies are known to exist; one is at the Library Company of Philadelphia.

43 Sifton, "Pierre Eugène Du Simitière," pp. 415-17.

44 Ibid., p. 417.

45 See Joel J. Orosz, "Pierre Eugène Du Simitière: Museum Pioneer in America." *Museum Studies Journal* I (Spring, 1985), pp. 11-14.

46 Ibid., p. 10. (The Congressman's name in this source is erroneously given as "William" Smith. His first name was, in fact, "Richard," and he was the brother of Du Simitière's late Patron, John Smith. See "John Smith" in *The National Cyclopedia of American Biography*, Vol. 13, p. 582.

47 Ibid., p. 14. For an excellent account of the articles contained within the American Museum, see "Pierre Eugène Du Simitière: His American Museum 200 Years After." Catalogue of an exhibition at the Library Company of Philadelphia, July-October, 1985.

48 Du Simitière, "Observations Sur Les Sauvages," *Du Simitière Papers*, Vol. III, Item 1f, Library Company of Philadelphia.

49 Du Simitière, *Scraps*, No. 92, Historical Society of Pennsylvania.

50 Du Simitière, "Spanish Antiquities: Coins," *Du Simitière Papers:* Vol. VI, 968.F.17a, Library Company of Philadelphia.

51 Du Simitière to Hon. William Fleming, Esq., September 26, 1779. Du Simitière, *Letterbook*, Peter Force Papers, Series 8D, Library of Congress.

52 Du Simitière to George Clinton, December 24, 1779. *Stauffer Collection*, Vol. 30, p. 2340, Historical Society of Pennsylvania.

53 Du Simitière, *Memoranda Book*, 1774-1783, Library of Congress. Also quoted, in its entirety, in Sifton, "Pierre Eugène Du Simitière," pp. 407-414.

54 Du Simitière to George Clinton, June 6, 1783. Du Simitière *Letterbook*, Peter Force Papers, Series 8D, Library of Congress.

55 Du Simitière to John Sullivan, July 2, 1783, Ibid.

56 See, for example, New Netherlands Co., Inc.'s *65th Unrestricted Public Auction Sale* (The Great Affleck-Ball Collection of Continental and Colonial Currency) December 3-4, 1975. Lots 312-29 are New Hampshire Revolutionary-Era Notes, while Lots 421-48 are emissions from the same period in New York.

57 John Christopher Kunze (1744-1807) was born in Saxony, and came to Philadelphia in 1770 to be a pastor in that city's Lutheran church. In 1784 he moved to New York to be pastor of Christ Church on Frankfort Street, a post he held until his death. According to his biographer, Kunze was a brilliant scholar, "a student also of medicine, astronomy, and numismatics." See George Harvey Genzmer, "John Christopher Kunze" in Dumas Malone, ed. *Dictionary of American Biography*, Vol. V (New York: Charles Scribner's Sons, 1932), pp. 512-13.

58 According to an early chronicler of the New-York Historical Society, "An extensive and valuable cabinet of coins and medals was presented to the Society, July 14, 1818, by the heirs of Rev. Dr. John C. Kunze...This collection was stolen from the Society a few years after its reception, nothing remaining but the cabinet which held the coins and medals." See Robert Hendre Kelby, *The New York Historical Society, 1804-1904* (New York: New-York Historical Society, 1905) p. 33.

59 Du Simitière, *Common Place Book*, Library of Congress: quoted in William John Potts, "Du Simitière, Artist, Antiquary, and Naturalist, Projector of the First American Museum, With Some Extracts from His Notebook," *Pennsylvania Magazine of History and Biography* 13 (October 1889), p. 360. "The Queen of Pamunkey" piece is listed as No. 45 in C. Willys Betts' *American Colonial History Illustrated by Contemporary Medals* (New York: Scott Stamp and Coin Co., Ltd., 1894), p. 26. Betts incorrectly rendered it as "Pamunky." The piece is actually not a struck medal, but rather a hand-wrought frontlet made to fasten to the front of a hat or coat. This is the conclusion of Harrold E. Gillingham, in his article "Early American Indian Medals," *Antiques* 6 (December 1924), p. 312. Gillingham supported his position by stating there are five loops on the reverse of the medal, and that when a specimen was presented to the Virginia Historical Society, it was fastened to a battered cloth cap. The piece is illustrated by Gillingham. It is an oval, 3¼ inches by 4¼ inches, with the arms of England engraved in the center, encircled in an upper oval, and an oblong beneath bears the legend "The Queen of Pamunkey." (See Gillingham, *Early American Indian Medals*, p. 312). Betts also noted a "King of Pamunkee" Medal (No. 46) and a "Ye King of Patomack" Medal (No. 47). The author is grateful to Michael Hodder of Bowers and Merena Galleries for research help on this piece. It is illustrated as fig. 4.

60 Du Simitière, *Memoranda Book*, 1774-1783, Library of Congress; quoted in Potts, "Du Simitière," p. 367.

61 See Betts, *Contemporary Medals*, p. 26 (Note 2).

62 See Gillingham, *Early American Indian Medals*, p. 312.

63 This piece was absent from both Bowers and Ruddy's *Garrett Collection Sales* (1979-1981), and from Bowers and Merena's *David W. Dreyfuss Sale* in 1986. Betts, writing in 1894, noted an example was in the collection of Dr. M.P. Scott of Baltimore. Gillingham in his *Early American Indian Medals*, p. 312, noted a specimen had been given to the Virginia Historical Society. This is incorrect, for as of this writing, the "medal" is the property of the Virginia Association of Antiquities, in Richmond. It is unclear if the Scott piece and the Virginia Association of Antiquities specimen are in fact the same frontlet. Gillingham also notes an odd misconception whereby this piece has been referred to as the "Pocahontas Frontlet," an inexplicable error since Charles II's reign began 43 years after Pocahontas' death. Du Simitière did own at least three Indian Peace Medals. According to entries in his *Common Place Book,* he purchased a copper medal with George I on the obverse (Betts 165), dating from the 1720s. His second Indian Medal was a silver striking with George III on the obverse and a wolf attacking a lion on the reverse (Betts 535); Betts attributed this medal to 1765-1766, while Du Simitière asserted that it was sent from England during the American Revolution. This particular medal, according to the Swiss, was "found among the plunder of Post St. Vincent by Col. [George Rogers] Clark of Virginia in 1779." The third medal was the notable "Rebellion to Tyrants is Obedience to God" obverse with "Happy While United" reverse (Betts 570), which was a gift from Col. Isaac Zane. See Potts, "Du Simitière," pp. 374-75.

64 Du Simitière, *Memoranda Book,* 1774-1783, Library of Congress; quoted in Potts, "Du Simitière," p. 363. Du Simitière may have been mistaken as to the dates, or the numbers could have referred to the subjects of the medals rather than the date of their manufacture.

65 Letter to the author from Gordon Marshall, Assistant Librarian, Library Company of Philadelphia, June 29, 1986. The author also wishes to thank Q. David Bowers and Michael Hodder of Bowers and Merena Galleries, Inc. for their research help on this subject.

66 C. Willys Betts later became a numismatic scholar of some distinction; in 1894 he authored *American Colonial History Illustrated by Contemporary Medals* (previously cited). The quote here given, and subsequent information on the Novum Belgium pieces (unless specifically cited to the contrary) is from Don Taxay, *Counterfeit, Mis-struck and Unofficial U.S. Coins* (New York: Arco Publishing, 1963), pp. 139-45.

67 See Ed. Frossard, *Numisma* I, (November 1877). Reprint edition, Ramm Communications, 1983.

68 Frossard's battle with J.W. Scott was by no means his only scrape with his fellow dealers. His long-term feud with W. Elliot Woodward has been well summarized in John W. Adams, "Woodward vs. Frossard" *The Asylum* I (Fall-Winter, 1980), pp. 27-32. Frossard's fisticuffs with Lyman Low is admirably recounted in Carl W.A. Carlson's "Strawberry Leaves and Shiners," *The Numismatist* 91 (November, 1978), pp. 2254-56.

69 Lyman H. Butterfield, Ed., *The Adams Papers. Series II: Adams Family Correspondence,* Vol. 2, June, 1776-March, 1778 (Cambridge: The Belknap Press of Harvard University, 1963), p. 96.

70 Lyman H. Butterfield, ed., *The Adams Papers. Series I: Diary and Autobiography of John Adams.* Four Vols., Vol. III: *Diary, 1782-1804* (Cambridge: Harvard University Press, 1961), p. 376 (Note).

71 Russell Rulau and George Fuld, *Medallic Portraits of Washington: Centennial Edition* (Iola, Wisconsin: Krause Publications, 1985), p. 52.

72 Richard S. Patterson and Richardson Dougall, *The Eagle and the Shield: A History of the Great Seal of the United States* (Washington, DC: U.S. Department of State, 1978), p. 6.

73 Ibid., p. 12. In addition to Virginia, Du Simitière had designed the seals for the states of Delaware and New Jersey, both of which are still in use today.

74 Lyman H. Butterfield, *Adams Family Correspondence,* Vol. 2, p. 96.

75 This unique piece appeared in Bowers and Ruddy's *Garrett Collection Sales,* I, November 28-29, 1979, Lot 574.

76 E Pluribus Unum (out of many, one) had been the motto of an English publication called *The Gentleman's Journal,* which had used this phrase from January 1692 to November 1694.

It then ceased publication, but the motto was picked up by the *Gentlemen's Magazine*, which was published in London from 1731 to 1922. Du Simitière, an inveterate reader, surely spied the legend on the title page of this publication. See Patterson and Dougall, *The Eagle and the Shield*, pp. 22-23.

77 *Symbolorvm et emblematvm ex volatilibus et insectis desvmtorvm centvria tertia, collecta a Ioachimo Camerario medico Norimberg* (A Third Century of Symbols and Emblems Chosen From Birds and Insects, Collected by Joachim Camerarius, Physician of Nuremberg). Benjamin Franklin dissented from the choice of the eagle as the nation's symbol on the grounds that it was a European scavenger. He preferred the wild turkey, an American bird that had, in his opinion, a noble aspect.

78 Thomson was enough of a collector to have preserved two of the earliest United States coins, the unique 1783 Nova Constellatio silver patterns for the Quint (500 units) and the Mark (1,000 units). Thomson locked these two coins into his desk; the desk and the coins within passed, by inheritance, to Thomson's nephew, and then to his nephew's son. The coins were eventually purchased by John Work Garrett of Baltimore. They were sold in Bowers and Ruddy's *Garrett Collection Sale* I, November 28-29, 1979, as Lots 620 and 622 respectively. Du Simitière included a listing of these patterns as number 20 in his "Historical Outline," quoted above. No doubt it was Thomson who provided the Swiss with a glimpse at the patterns. For a brief history of the Nova Constellatio patterns and Thomson's involvement with them, see *Garrett* I, pp. 149-53, and Bowers, *U.S. Coinage*, pp. 134-35.

79 Du Simitière, *Memoranda Book*, 1774-1783, Library of Congress, quoted in Sifton, "Pierre Eugène Du Simitière," pp. 408-410.

80 Yeoman, *Guide Book of United States Coins*, 40th edition, p. 24. Mention should be made of the fact that generic information from the *Guide Book*, although not always specifically cited, has proved invaluable in the preparation of this article.

81 For the full story of Thomson and the Seal, see Patterson and Dougall, *The Eagle and the Shield*, pp. 93-101.

82 Du Simitière, *Common Place Book*, Library of Congress; quoted in Potts, "Du Simitière," p. 359.

83 The original roster of portraits included Washington, Baron Von Steuben, John Jay, Henry Laurens, Charles Thomson, Horatio Gates, Gouverneur Morris, Samuel Huntingdon, Silas Deane, William H. Drayton, John Dickinson, Joseph Reed, Benedict Arnold, and Thomas Mifflin. See Edna Donnell, "Portraits of Eminent Americans After Drawings by Du Simitière," *Antiques* 24 (July 1933), p. 19. See also Potts, "Du Simitière," p. 343.

84 Du Simitière, *Common Place Book*, Library of Congress; quoted in Donnell, "Portraits," p. 17.

85 No such print of Gerard is found in the print departments of either the Metropolitan Museum of Art in New York City, or in the *Bibliotheque Nationale*, Paris. As for the Mifflin portrait, Du Simitière recalled it from Gerard a scant six days after handing it over, on the grounds it was "not fit to be engraven." Quoted in Donnell, "Portraits," p. 18. Apparently, it was never replaced.

86 For the best account of Du Simitière's tribulations, see Donnell, "Portraits," pp. 17-21.

87 Du Simitière, *Letterbook*, 1779-1784, Library of Congress; quoted in Donnell, "Portraits," p. 20.

88 Baker said Du Simitière settled in Philadelphia in 1766, when in fact it was 1774; he speculated that Du Simitière's Washington Portrait was done in pencil or water colors, when in fact it was black lead; and Baker guessed the portrait was drawn in the winter of 1778-1779, when it was actually drawn on February 1, 1779. See W.S. Baker, *Medallic Portraits of Washington* (Philadelphia: Robert M. Lindsay, 1885; Reprint edition, Iola, Wisconsin: Krause Publications, 1965), p. 10.

89 Rulau and Fuld, *Medallic Portraits*, previously cited.

90 Walter Breen and Anthony Swiatek, *The Encyclopedia of United States Silver and Gold Commemorative Coins, 1892-1954* (New York: Arco Publishing, Inc., 1981), p. 123. Rulau and Fuld do not say, however, from which source Barber took his model. If Du Simitière's drawing was that source, the Swiss would then have had a hand in the first official United States coin carrying the bust of Washington.

91 Baker, *Medallic Portraits*, pp. 10-11.

92 See Donnell, "Portraits," pp. 17-18.

93 It is possible that Du Simitière influenced the design of two other coins, the Washington Dollars of 1794 and 1796 (Baker 28 and 33). The plate specimen given in Rulau and Fuld is, however, too worn to make a positive identification. Neither Baker nor Rulau and Fuld mention this possibility. See Rulau and Fuld, *Medallic Portraits*, p. 38. Nearly all of the varieties mentioned above are plated in this important text, making it indispensable to this work.

94 Du Simitière to Conrad Alexander Gerard, September 12, 1782. Du Simitière *Letterbook*, Peter Force Papers, Series 8D, Library of Congress.

95 For the full story of Jefferson and Du Simitière, see Orosz, "Pierre Eugène Du Simitière," pp. 15-18.

96 Ibid., p. 15.

97 Quoted in Hans Huth, "Pierre Eugène Du Simitière and the Beginnings of the American Historical Museum," *Pennsylvania Magazine of History and Biography* 69 (October 1945), p. 321. Hazard did attempt to sell the collection *en bloc* to the American Philosophical Society, but he withdrew his offer when the A.P.S. expressed interest in only a few parts of it. See "200 Years After," p. 38.

98 Attinelli, *Numisgraphics*, p. 5. See also the frontispiece, a facsimile of the Watkin broadside.

99 "For Sale at Public Vendue ... The American Museum," (March 10, 1785). Broadside in the Collection of the Library Company of Philadelphia.

100 George Frederick Kolbe, *The Numismatic Bookseller* 2 (September 1985), p. 1.

101 Charles Willson Peale to Ebenezer Hazard, July 26, 1787. *Peale Papers*, American Philosophical Society.

102 Ebenezer Hazard to Thomas Bradford, February 17, 1790. *Bradford Collection*, Historical Society of Pennsylvania.

103 John Connelly, Advertisement of Sale of the Estate of Matthew Clarkson, *Poulson's American Daily Advertiser*, No. 7446, October 29, 1800. See also "200 Years After," p. 39. Although it is pure speculation, there are two candidates for purchaser. Major James was probably deceased by 1800, and Rev. Andrew Eliot had died in 1778. However, James Winthrop (1752-1821) and William Bentley (1759-1819) were active numismatists in 1800. Winthrop came from an illustrious family—his father was the celebrated astronomer, physicist, and mathematician, John Winthrop, and James was directly descended from John Winthrop, the first governor of Massachusetts Bay—and was in his own right a notable librarian and jurist. Bentley was a Unitarian clergyman in Salem who kept a voluminous diary, published in four volumes by the Essex Institute in 1905-14. The diaries cover the years from 1784 to 1819, and detail many numismatic activities by both

Bentley and his friend, Winthrop. It is possible—but by no means probable—that Bentley or Winthrop was the purchaser. Excerpts from the Bentley diaries that specifically relate to numismatics were reprinted in: George Heath, ed. "Oldest Coin Collection Recorded in the U.S.", *The Numismatist* 20 (January, 1907), pp. 10-12. The author is grateful to Eric P. Newman for research help on this subject.

104 Charles Willson Peale, *Autobiography* (1826), p. 99. Previously cited.

INDEX

The Eagle That Is Forgotten